How To Book Acting Jobs in TV and Film

The Truth About the Acting Industry -

Conversations With a Veteran Hollywood

Casting Director

SECOND EDITION

by
Cathy Reinking, CSA

for Kate Marie Reinking

Reviews from First Edition

Blessing to Actors!, June 12, 2012
by Great, the Alexander
"This is a great education coming from a Pro, well established and fresh in the business! Why CDs think and act the way they do. Etiquette in the room, Agencies worth noting, Even hotspots in LA Night Life!! She writes so that you feel like you're actually in front of her, having a conversation. I met Cathy shortly after reading her book for the first time and can testify, there is nothing fake about her! She represents everything she teaches and thus practices what she preaches. In her book she talks about loving actors who are genuinely great people inside. She is this, in the form of a casting director and educator.
There is SO much valuable information in this book for actors with all levels of experience. I keep it with my audition materials and handy for inspiration. Read this book, re-read, and use it as a reference. It will change your life, or at least your acting career for the better!"

A Must Read! May 13, 2011
By Karen D'Amico
"This book is a must read for everyone in the entertainment business. Eye opening, educating, and straight talk from someone in the business who "knows". Actors should not go to one more audition without reading this book!"

Cutthroat Advice! October 7, 2010
By Brian McClure
"Cathy's No Holds Barred approach to this process was clever and eye opening. There's nothing sugar coated here and that's just as it should be. READ NOW!"

A Serious Book for Serious Actors, May 23, 2010
Jeffrey N. Fritz "Nikon Jeff" (Morgantown, West Virginia) -
"Call it coincidence, but less than a week after reading this book I had three auditions and landed a role in a major play. No, this book won't guarantee you a role or an acting career. However, if you take the suggestions from a highly successful casting director to heart and apply them, you will be the better off for it.
The book is engaging and an easy read. You gain a fresh and important view from the other side of "The Room." You see what the casting director sees and understand what the producer is looking for from the talent in "The Room." Nearly all aspects of acting are covered from television to film to theater. Even subtle differences in comedy and dramatic TV are covered.
If you are serious about acting on any level this is your book."

One book you DON"T skip, January 26, 2010
D. Yee "down to earth" (Boston, MA) -
"Anyone within the Industry of Film, yet alone just Actors, would be sadly mistaken if they do not read this book cover to cover. The wealth of information coming from someone that is be your biggest Ally is amazingly jaw dropping, regardless of your level of experience. It will motivate you like nothing else.
Also, I finished the book in 2 days, I just couldn't set it down. You will not be sorry."

no more, no less...just right, August 30, 2009
Sam Stevens "glorfindel" (los angeles)
"As someone who has coached actors for film and television auditions in Los Angeles for the last 14 years, I can honestly say Cathy's book says it all! Everything you need to know about what to expect, and everything you need to improve your auditioning skills

4

immediately, is in this book. I also love the fact that there is no extraneous B.S! She keeps it simple and clear with no confusing and useless information. Too many "how to' books about the business "talk too much' and give actors directives that do nothing but confound the process. I highly recommend Cathy's book to every actor auditioning, or thinking about auditioning for film and television anywhere in the world. I would also recommend it to every acting teacher and coach as well!"

Table of Contents

Reinking

Time To Update or Welcome To The Digital Age

Almost twenty years ago, when I started casting in TV and film, the job description for a Casting Director was basically "must love and know actors. TV and film watching from an early age a plus. Great organizational skills and good with people." Today, this job description is typical: "Someone who is highly efficient, with both Casting Associate skills and office management and administrative skills; someone who is a speedy and efficient multi-tasker, extremely detail oriented, an expert speller, extremely organized, and fun. Duties include (but are not limited to) making lists, running sessions, creating budgets, managing all projects (both in development and production), maintaining avail grids, creating picture boards, editing video, managing video database, and the overall management of the entire casting department. We need someone who is willing to work long hours. Must be a MAC user. Must have expert skills in the following computer programs: Microsoft Word, Excel, iMovie, iDVD, Cast It, and Breakdown Express. Knowledge of Outlook and PowerPoint a big plus."

Welcome to TV, film, and commercial casting.

I wrote and published the first edition of this book in 2009. It's now 2012 and so much has changed in the casting business that a second edition is needed.

Although the title suggests a "how-to" manual about getting a job, the core "how-to" here is *How To Emotionally Connect with People.* Connecting emotionally with others and especially yourself - being in tune with who you are and possessing self-knowledge - are the basic precepts of this book and, in my opinion, to becoming a better human being. If you can master emotional connections with others and strive for self-knowledge, then you will just naturally be a better actor. If you can improve your life as an actor, you will master The Room.

In this edition, I amplify the basic points of the book – the critical notion of charisma and what casting directors are looking for – with detailed descriptions of the audition process and the various styles of auditioning for each type of TV show, film, and commercial.

What constitutes great acting and what makes for a great audition have not changed. What has changed, and pretty substantially, is the technology within the Industry in general and within the casting world specifically. And the digital age has not only changed what I do and what tools I need to do my job, but it's changed the tools and skills that an actor needs as well. For instance, a casting director now needs to own a video camera and have the know-how to download, edit, and upload the videos we create. The same holds for actors, who more often than not will now self-submit, or "go on tape" in the privacy of their own home.

Another technological breakthrough that makes our lives so much easier is the whole electronic submission process. Virtually all submissions are now electronic, via Breakdown Services. Years after I began we continued to use hard copy submissions for all our projects, which our office received through mail and delivery literally by the bucketful. When I was starting out as a casting intern, one of my jobs was to open each manila envelope that held a headshot and resume and put them in stacks according to the roles. For a pilot, it would take me days to complete this task. (Thank God we are now more eco-friendly.)

This new edition explores the pros and cons of these technological advances. This will help you better understand them from the perspective of the casting director and alter how you do things.

I also brought in some special guests. In keeping with the tone of this book, I have interviewed four very successful working actors, of diverse ages, gender, backgrounds, and training, and our conversations are captured for you to read.

Amy Pietz ("The Office," "Caroline in the City"), Sarah Drew (Dr. April Kepner on "Grey's Anatomy"), Madeline Zima ("Californication," *Crazy Eyes*), and Mark J. Sullivan (regional theatre work at The Old Globe and others, "Kindle Friends" Guy). While they all have enviable careers, they also are articulate, intelligent, very sweet and possess charisma: Four qualities I always look for in actors. I am grateful for their generosity of spirit in sharing with me their experiences in The Room and I believe their insight helps deepen the understanding of what it truly means to be a working actor (and book those precious acting jobs!).

I would also like to thank a special group of young actresses - Joy Caldwell, Kelli Rasmus, and Kenya Alexander - who helped me understand the issues related specifically to non-white females entering the profession today from their perspective. Their candor and passion are an inspiration to me.

What I want to make clear in this edition is that there aren't any "entry level" positions in the world of casting for network and cable TV or studio films. We have to populate these shows and films with the best-of-the-best. We don't think to ourselves, oh, so-and-so isn't that great, let's bring them in for a co-star role. In fact, most of the actors we bring in for those roles are overqualified. We find work for actors and all the actors we want to find work for are excellent. Bottom line. This is especially true on prestige shows like "Grey's Anatomy," "How I Met Your Mother," and the like. On "Frasier," the writer/producers used to deliberate for hours on which actor they liked best for the role of a waiter whose only line was "Would you like foam with your cappuccino?" But this standard is also true in all the other types of projects I've cast; low-budget independently produced films in Los Angeles and in smaller markets, USC student films, commercials, new media including webseries, and theatre. Our bosses - the producers, directors, executives, ad agency clients - are all very hard to please, and we are always in the crosshairs. Please heed all the advice in this book. It's critical you do so for both the casting directors and for yourself!

In truth, we don't need more actors in Los Angeles or New York. We need more great actors.

But before you doing anything else, check out my favorite websites for the Business:

• DEADLINE HOLLYWOOD (sign up immediately for email notices! It's FREE.) Nikki Finke is the real deal and her website is much better than the old traditional "trades" such as Variety or The Hollywood Reporter)

• imdb.com (sign up for IMDB Pro)
• Backstage
• RottenTomatoes.com
• The Futon Critic (Current TV News)

My favorite films about the business of auditioning and the world of performing are the following:

Every Little Step
First Position
ShowBusiness
All That Jazz

And my favorite resource for the most current trends is a radio show entitled *The Business* , hosted by respected entertainment industry journalist Kim Masters of the Hollywood Reporter and produced by Darby Maloney at KCRW 89.9. Each week The Business features an analysis of top Hollywood news with John Horn of the Los Angeles Times, in-depth interviews and the occasional feature story.

In the digital version of this book, Darby Maloney has graciously allowed me to include an episode of the show on the subject of pilot season in this new edition. For you print readers, I suggest you go to the website www.kcrw.com and find the page for *The Business.*

Why I Wrote This Book?

This book is not a typical textbook for actors. Its tone is conversational, like chatting with a casting director about acting, auditioning, and surviving "The Room." The Room, which you will return to again and again as an actor, is as intense as it is intimate. I've been there with thousands of people. Most of them clearly lacked the advantage of talking with an experienced casting director who could share the secrets of The Room. Now, with this book, you have the opportunity to learn from one.

My decades in film, television and theatre have involved acting, writing, directing and teaching. I spent the majority of that time, however, as a Casting Director on many movies, TV series, and pilots including "Arrested Development," "According to Jim," and eight seasons of "Frasier." For part of that time I was the Manager of Casting at NBC.

I loved my work, and each day that I found, recommended, coached and cast actors, I felt that I was quietly repaying a personal debt owed since childhood. I offer this book as a final balloon payment that I hope will lift actors – young and old, novice and experienced – into The Room and beyond.

What energized me through the endless days in The Room, nights in taping, and weekends in theatres, was the fact that I simply love actors. I've gladly devoted my life to watching and working with them. It's a love – idolizing, really – that began at a very young age.

As a two-year-old I would perform in front of a huge, wall-sized mirror in my living room. My self-motivated performing wasn't for a specific audience, mind you, but just for me. My childhood was chaotic. My father had survived the Holocaust only to be unable to survive real life. He was in and out of hospitals from the time I was five and then died at age forty-nine when I was twelve. I learned the hard way how much a girl needs her Dad during her teen years to boost her self-esteem when it comes to relationships with boys. Back then I just stumbled along out of touch.

My survival was to lose myself in plays and movies. The year my dad died, I saw *The Poseidon Adventure* at least eleven times, way before videotapes and DVDs. If you wanted to see a movie, you had to go to a theatre where it was showing. That was the only place I wanted to be. I was home in the dark, staring up at the screen where actors generously revealed what it was I was feeling. In the dark, I could laugh or cry openly.

Perhaps because of that relationship with actors and storytelling, I pursued a degree in theatre arts at UC Los Angeles. With my B.A., I've always stayed in the arts, completing the creative writing program at the University of Kansas, and being on staff at South Coast Repertory Theatre. I won awards as a screenwriter and directed and stage managed critically acclaimed theatrical productions, including many world premieres, in California, Colorado, Oregon, and Kansas.

Currently, I am the casting director at L.A. Theatre Works. A non-profit organization created in the 1980s by the inexhaustible and brilliant Susan Albert Loewenberg, LATW's mission is to present, preserve, and disseminate classic and contemporary plays in audio form. In a way, I've come full circle with my love for all things theatrical after a 15-year detour of all things in front of a camera.

I also teach acting and audition techniques in workshops throughout the U.S. and Canada.

Throughout it all, my devotion – and debt – to actors has only grown deeper. I hope this book will empower actors to pursue their truest course in life.

Some of the individuals I acknowledge for their advice, support, and encouragement, are listed below.

Beaty Reynolds, my writing mentor and exquisite friend. Thank you for encouraging me to write this book and going over the first draft with me sentence by sentence.

Jeff Greenberg, who was the casting director on "Frasier" for its eleven-year run. He gave me my big break into casting, and we worked side by side as his associate for eight of those years. He changed my life. There would be no book if it were not for him and all he taught and shared with me.

Julie Haber, for being a generous friend for years and introducing me to Jeff.

Marc Hirschfeld, for hiring me as Manager of Casting at NBC and being a great person with exquisite taste in actors.

All the agents in Los Angeles and New York. You are the unsung heroes.

All the actors, of course. Can't make movies, television, and theatre without you!

Cris Gross, the best, most steadfast friend I have had – at 31 years and counting. This book couldn't have been published without you.

The last shall be first . . . my daughter, Kate Marie Reinking, who gave up so much for my career. My love for you surpasses all the love I have for actors.

chapter one

What's It Like In The Room?

The audition room is a very odd place. The Room, and your presence in it, are critical aspects of securing a job. The Room is not an easy place to master. It's usually someone's office, sometimes a conference room, and in no way simulates a set, a sound stage or being on location. You'll most likely not be acting your scene with another actor, and you'll definitely not have weeks of rehearsal time to get it perfect, as you would in a scheduled play.

You have to be completely present, in the moment, likable and charismatic, with the phones in the outer office ringing off the hook and twenty to thirty actors waiting for you to finish your audition.

Mastering the audition is a huge part of being a working actor, and it isn't easy. If you can't audition well, you won't get the chance to be in a cool film that premieres at Sundance or have your own trailer on the Paramount lot. Mastering the audition is about you being able to reveal your charisma in all its beauty within a nanosecond (dare I say "blink") of entering that room.

If you can't reveal your charisma in The Room, you won't book the job. The writer, producers, and directors who sit in on the callbacks are those parental figures you can never please. You'll never be good enough – they'll find the oddest things to fault you on (shirt is wrinkled, too much attitude, etc.)

However, when you're able to master The Room, when you're able to reveal to the casting director, producer, or director who you really are – your natural charisma and individual humanity in all its beautiful rawness – they'll adore you as only the best lovers can. They'll make you a star and you'll make their work (especially the writing) better than it is.

In The Room, that unglamorous, unromantic box with no set, no costumes, no lights, no hair and make-up people, and no other actors except yourself, you must make them fall in love with you.

My heart goes out to you.

During my years as a casting director for episodic TV, I had the great fortune to have worked on not just one but two Emmy® Award-winning TV Shows, "Frasier " and "Arrested Development."

Every actor who utters even one line on any film or TV show you watch . . . all those hundreds, thousands of people who make a living as actors . . . had to impress a casting director. We are the keepers of the gate and we are constantly looking for exceptional actors, and, if we're lucky, the next big star to lead through that gate.

I am a fan of actors. During the eight years I worked on "Frasier" I was able to meet and work not only with the brilliant regular cast of the show – Kelsey Grammer, David Hyde Pierce, John Mahoney, Peri Gilpin, Jane Leeves, Dan Butler, Edward Hibbert, Tom McGowan – but also with a parade of incredible guest stars. These included James Earl Jones, Sir Derek Jacobi, Eva Marie Saint, Michael Keaton, Teri Hatcher, Virginia Madsen, and Jean Smart to name just a few. Then there were the hundreds of future stars who came in to my auditions when they were "unknown." For some – Dakota Fanning, Jessica Alba, Eva Mendez, Sandra Oh, Chad Michael Murray, and Erica Christiansen – it was one of their very first auditions. These, and thousands of good working actors, came in on a daily basis to audition for all the speaking roles on "Frasier" and the other shows and films I worked on concurrently. I touched so many lives and helped give so many worthy actors their first big break. I was there at all the audition sessions, the table reads, the rehearsals, the shoot nights, the parties, the martinis, for many, many years.

This meant thousands upon thousands of hours spent in The Room. I am an expert on The Room. All casting directors are. Actors do not fully understand The Room. Directors and producers do not fully understand The Room. I can't tell you how many actors I championed after seeing brilliant work on stage or in a small independent ("indie") film only to then have them come into the audition room and tank. For some reason, they did not show the very charisma I had already seen for myself in a different context. There are a lot of frustrating hours in The Room for those of us rooting for our favorite actors, those who have truly moved us. If the director or producer or whomever is the decision maker in this process does not see or experience "the goods" in The Room they cannot be convinced otherwise. If we push our case too much, they will feel railroaded and if we do convince them, they will resent it in the long run.

The room is not only frustrating, it is boring. For a typical primetime network and cable TV pilot, we'll see 300 actors per role. In a pilot that has six to fifteen series regulars, that means hearing the same material over and over again until we'd rather poke our eyes out than hear the same scene one more time. Sometimes the material is brilliant and sometimes, not so much, but even the most brilliant material gets old after the hundredth reading. Now multiply that by ten.

Also know that the project – whether it's a TV show or a film or even a commercial – is always the number one concern, not your feelings, your time, or your career. The folks that hire you might fall in love with you, but they don't really care about you that much. Just know that going in and you won't get your heart broken.

Please don't go into The Room seeking approval. The room is all about booking a job so you can practice your craft as an actor. The good actors share their talent with an audience. Fulfilling your dreams is not really why you should go into the acting profession and it certainly won't fix what ails you. Dealing with your personal issues through therapy or a spiritual journey will make you feel better, not the adoration of people you don't know.

If you're a healthy actor, what are the unspoken rules of The Room? These rules I refer to are not known by agents or acting coaches; otherwise, you wouldn't hear advice like "make bold choices" or "take your time before you start the audition - it's all about you and your time." Comments like these – given to actors with all good intentions – make me nervous. They lack a basic understanding of The Room

The Rules of the Room

The audition begins as soon as you're in the vicinity of the building. You never know when you might run into the casting director or writer/producers who will be running your audition. That it is why it is essential to begin projecting a good, positive attitude the moment you get out of your car or walk through the front gate.

The writer/producer is running to the audition (they're always late and frantic) and comes in contact with the actors outside on the sidewalk or in the waiting room. Writer/producers are sensitive and perceptive sorts, and if you treat them differently after you know who they are, they will mentally take note of that and penalize you for it. Be positive and nice to everyone outside of The Room.

By the way, this is a good time to explain that in TV the writer is a producer as well. They not only write the episodes but they help in the creation of each program. They are considered writer/producers and they rule. In film, the director rules. A producer in films is very different than a producer in TV.

The first round of auditions are usually just with the casting director. The session is called a "pre-read." We will choose the best actors from this preliminary session to go to the "callback." In TV, the callback is the "producer's session" and in film, the callback is the "director's session."

So you arrive at the pre-read session, sign in on a SAG-AFTRA sheet that is placed in the waiting area, and take a seat. Don't visit or talk with the other actors in the waiting area. You will be tempted, especially when you start to know and like a lot of your fellow actors, to share war stories or catch up with them on a social level. You don't want to come off as unfriendly or stuck up, right? Just be polite and refrain from visiting. Concentrate on your task at hand. Use this precious time to focus, meditate, and run through your material. Remember, the audition is the work for the actor. Each audition is precious and you should treat it as such, no matter how many you go on or how many years you've been doing it.

I knew a girl whose parents sacrificed a lot of time and money for her to be in Los Angeles and work as a young actress. She was quite good and was able to make an adjustment in her performance when she was focused. Her issue as an actress was that she tended to be a bit too perky for most directors/producers' tastes. Her manager had properly coached her in preparation for an audition for a very serious scene in a studio film. However, while she was waiting to go in to the audition, she was playing with a couple of the other young actresses – talking, making up stories – basically, being an outgoing, happy ten-year-old. She was not concentrating on the scene or the emotional life of the character. When her name was called, she entered The Room a happy and perky kid, exactly what she was told by her manager not to be. This was a juicy role in a prestigious, serious film. Word got back to her manager that she was not focused and much too animated for the role. The manager told the agent, and then the agent was reluctant to send her in for any more roles.

It's very tough for an agent to get an audition for an unknown. The agent and manager both put their reputations and taste on the line. Once an actor blows an audition, they get put on the "too risky" list. With the time, money, and emotion spent getting in the door, you can't blow one audition. This is a serious business. You need to be ready to do the scene as soon as your name is called to enter The Room. There is no prep or warm up once you're in The Room. Your prep and warm up time is in the waiting room.

Have your headshot and resumé (already stapled together) with you as you're waiting in the waiting room. Your pic and res, as we call them, must be ready to hand to the casting director when requested, which is usually with the first greeting. Don't assume the casting director already has your materials in hand. Even if they do, they still need an artifact with which to remember you by and to help organize the session as a whole. If they don't have a hard copy pic and res of you in The Room, you run the risk of being forgotten.

Always have a set on your person, not in your purse or briefcase. The time you take to retrieve your purse or briefcase and find these items is wasted time and wasted time is irritating to the casting director. Have it on you so you hand it over in one simple move. Don't have your resumé separate from your headshot, in which case you or the casting director will have to take the time to get a stapler and staple them together. Irritating.

Casting directors are very impatient people. We have so many folks breathing down our necks – directors, producers, network and studio executives, agents, actors – and goodness knows what personal issues we have at any given moment. This all might seem silly, mundane, and have nothing whatsoever to do with acting or doing good work, but trust me, it makes a difference to our opinion of you. The audition location is like a factory of acting; we have to get actors in and out very quickly because we have to see a lot of folks in one session. We can't waste precious time waiting for you to get yourself together.

Honestly, sometimes we just don't have the time to be forgiving, generous, and nice when you don't have your act together. We help you out by bringing you in for the audition and giving you an opportunity to act. You can help us out by bringing your "A" game always.

Okay, so you've parked your car, waited in the waiting area, your name has been called, and you (finally!) enter The Room, with your headshot and resumé stapled together.

Always bring your "sides" (the material for the audition) in with you. Casting directors get nervous when we see you without your sides. We either think, "damn it, they didn't get their sides and they aren't prepared," or "damn it, this cocky actor thinks he's so memorized, he doesn't need his sides anymore."

You do not get points for memorizing. Remember, it's an audition not a performance. You can refer back to your sides if you need to during the actual reading. The main thing is to keep the audition moving. It's worse to "go up" (forget your lines) than it is to look down at your sides for the next line. When you go up you get disconnected from the character and the person you're reading with. When you have to look down, you can do so quickly and keep the scene flowing.

So you enter The Room, all ready to go with your sides and headshot and resumé. Either the casting director greets you at the door, or you're brought in by the assistant or associate and introduced to the casting director. Don't put your hand out to shake the casting director's hand unless he or she extends their hand first. Let the casting director guide you on manners. Some casting directors have issues with germs because we see a lot of people in one day. If we have eight hours of auditions in a single day, we might see 200-plus actors that day. If we shake every person's hand, that's a hell of a lot of germs. We come in contact with more human bodies then even a schoolteacher, perhaps as much as politicians on the campaign trail. We're not necessarily paranoid (although some of us might be) but we're practical. Plus, it's an audition, not a job interview, therefore, no handshaking unless the casting director initiates it.

Don't come in and want to chat before the actual reading begins. Again, let the casting director be your guide in the manners of The Room. If we want to chat with you then you can chat. Maybe we'll ask you about something on your resumé or mention a play we just saw you in. Don't come into The Room and gush about the show, the drive over to the audition, or us. This is extraneous and sucks up precious time. Just come in as the most natural "you" possible, say "Hi," and be ready to sit or stand in place and begin.

This early in the audition, before it's even really started, the casting director has already decided whether they like you or not. Most auditioners are assessed through the eyes and by the way you walk, stand, and sit. Are your eyes clear and alive? Or are they murky and full of fear and uncertainty? Are you stiff, physically? Are you relaxed with a natural posture? Do we feel comfortable being around you? It is your job to make us comfortable, not the other way around. We must sense that you can handle yourself in any situation, especially on a set, which is not the most forgiving environment in the world. You think it's tough in The Room? Well, the set is pure chaos with a lot of insecure people running around counting on you, the actor, to know what you're doing. You must reflect a reassuring confidence the moment you enter and take your seat.

Please don't ask the following questions of the casting director:

"What are you looking for?"

"What are you not finding in the other actors?"

"Should I be natural or more 'charactery?'"

"I prepared three versions. Which one would you like me to do first?"

"What is my relationship to the lead actor?"

These might be fine questions in a different context, like at a job interview or in a play rehearsal, but not in The Room. These questions reek of "actor" in the negative connotation of the word. We (and the directors) don't want to see the wheels turning – we don't want to see you working. We want you to come into The Room focused and owning The Room, not needy or insecure, like a deer in headlights. What are we looking for? We are always looking for "you" in the scene and for you to be brilliant and interesting.

Whatever questions you might have can be answered ahead of time by either the "breakdown" or the information/ exposition gleaned directly from the dialogue and action in the scene. Sometimes, concocting an elaborate "back story" (the characters history) that's not found directly in the script - adding an incest twist where there is none or making the character an exchange student from Germany - can ruin the audition.

Sometimes a casting director will ask you if you have any questions, as it's just a good neutral icebreaker to get the process rolling. The best answer to that question is "No."

Don't ever say, "I just got these sides." Even if true and your audition is suffering because of it, never say this. It makes everyone look bad – you, your agent (for getting you the sides late), and the casting director (for getting the sides to the agent late). There are never any excuses for being underprepared. And if there are somewhat legitimate reasons, we don't want to hear them.

The Reading Begins

The first thing you should do is connect with the reader/ casting director in every way you can. Most of the times, you will be reading with the casting director (although sometimes there is a "reader" so the casting director can just sit back and watch). What you don't want to do is heedlessly begin, barreling through the material. You don't want to just read the lines and, conversely, you don't want to, heaven forbid, overact. Relax and make great eye contact, revealing right off the bat your charisma. You must fall in love with the person you're doing the scene with. Just look in their eyes and find their humanity. Not an easy task, especially if the casting director is looking down at their sides, glancing at your resumé, or appearing to be irritated, tired or both. Don't get sucked into our energy! Make us get sucked into yours. Make your two eyes laser beams and bore into the casting director's eyes. I'm not saying make your eyes unnaturally big and look at us like an adoring fan, I'm just saying connect human to human. Make it about us, just as with any scene, whether it is in a film, on TV, or in a play. It's not about you and/or how you're doing, it's about the other person.

The hard fact is that you will hardly ever do an audition with another actor, especially not in television. You have got to learn to make it work with the non-actor before you. With film auditions, if you get a callback, you will probably have a "chemistry read" to assess the connection you have with another actor, but only if you're up for the lead. If your scene is with Brad Pitt and you're a day player, then no, Brad will not be doing a chemistry read with you. With pilot auditions, you might, if you're really lucky and up for a leading part, get to do your final audition for network with another actor. This means that you and an actor up for the lead opposite you audition in front of the network executives who are producing the show. But if you're auditioning for a supporting role, you're on your own. You might not meet all your fellow actors on a project until the first rehearsal when cast, crew, director, creators, and producers gather for a "table read" (the first read through of the script once all the roles are cast). All the more reason for you to find chemistry with the casting director any way you can. We are all you have at this point.

If you drop the momentum of the scene by going up or botching up a word or a line – try to keep going as if nothing were wrong. If the casting director wants to stop you at this point, we will, but if we don't stop you, just keep going.

The best auditions are smooth and easy. You have a strong connection, make good eye contact, and you keep it moving. If you're present in the moment, revealing your true self, and you don't need to correct yourself or start over, you will make the casting director very happy. If you absolutely must start over, it's imperative that you do a brilliant job the second time around. Once you have messed up, you have gotten yourself in a hole, and it is difficult to climb out of it entirely. Don't dig yourself a bigger hole by messing up again and apologizing too much. You might salvage the audition if you're flawless the second go-round, but even then you're on shaky ground.

Remember, there is no real rehearsal time on the set and we have to feel confident that we can "send you to the stage."

The more you're prepared with the material, the more relaxed you will be. The more relaxed you are, the more you'll be able to have good eye contact and connect with us. We're just looking for a connection like everyone else. We're looking for your humanity within the context of the scene, not your acting.

When the reading is done, the casting director will say something like "That's it. Thank you so much." They also might say "excellent," or "that's all you have to do," or "very nice." This is all meaningless. Not to say that it's empty praise, but this is not feedback on which to hang your hat. If you get a callback, then you did very well. If you don't get a callback, then you didn't impress us. Most of the time, that's all the feedback you will get. There just isn't time for the casting director to critique every actor.

I give very direct feedback to actors I know on a personal basis or to those whom I want to help out if there's time, but it's not our job in The Room to teach you to be a better actor. Our job is to find good actors for the shows and films we work on. We are beholden to the people who hire us. We love actors, but we simply don't have the time to give you everything. Don't become bitter toward us because of this fact.

If you go on a lot of auditions and don't get called back, don't convince yourself "they're just not looking for my type." The fault might lie with you. Don't expect us to answer the question that will live eternally at the back of your mind, no matter how confident, trained and experienced you are. "Do I have what it takes to make it as an actor?" We will never tell you point blank "that sucks," or "you should give up being an actor right now," or "you have absolutely no sex appeal whatsoever." We won't tell you. We can't tell. We don't have the insight and power for that. I've seen incredibly weak actors, whom I thought didn't have a prayer, learn from their bad auditions, improve over time, and end of up working a lot. I've seen actors perform brilliantly in either a play or a film, but then tank in The Room. As long as you're willing to get help where you need it, outside of The Room, then you will eventually master it.

Your audition is over and the casting director says, "Thank you very much." Don't, under any circumstance, continue the audition by saying, "Would you like to see it another way?" or "I can be directed." You're showing your desperate actor side by saying anything other than "thank you." If we want to see it another way, we'll ask for it. We know you can be directed, you're an actor for goodness sake! Simply leave. Don't sulk out defeated or storm out angry, just graciously exit.

Once you leave The Room, forget about the audition. Don't brood over it, don't relive it over and over in your distraught mind, and don't try to figure out how you could have done it differently or better. Forget about it! Effortlessly move on to the next task at hand.

Never get in your car, drive away, think about a new way to do the scene, then drive back to the audition room and ask to do it again. I've had this happen many times, and it's just embarrassing and uncomfortable. If the casting director wants to be nice, agreeing to let you do it again, you're now in a hole you can never climb out of because it's massive. You'll waste everyone's time. Just leave it alone at the first "thank you very much."

"Going On Tape"

One of the elements that has really changed in the last three years is that most if not all casting directors are "putting actors on tape" for the pre-read. In all the years I worked on sitcoms, we never used a video camera in the room. Now, you can't be a casting director without one. Who could have predicted that the casting director of 2012 would need to have the skills of a filmmaker?

Just as it is for the live auditions, we are not putting you on tape in the ideal of circumstances. We don't shoot you on a set with hair, make-up and professional quality lighting provided. We are not capturing you with the Red One digital camera. The technology we often use is very simple so to be cost effective. Because the footage we take is raw, it's even more crucial than ever that your auditions stand out.

The presence of the camera in The Room changes the dynamic of the interaction between actor and casting director. It makes it harder for an actor to emotionally connect with the material and with the reader. Sometimes you have to stand a certain way in front of a wall or screen, which might feel awkward and self-conscious. Questions might float in your mind like "where do I look? At the reader or directly into the camera?" This will of course avert your concentration from the task at hand, which is to be attractive and draw us in. What's an actor to do?

We tape all the pre-reads and then assess whose auditions we're going to forward to the client. Producers, directors, and ad agency clients alike prefer watching auditions remotely, from their device of choice, in their own time. The new technology has been a boon for these busy people, who used to have to sit through four to six hours of live auditions, taking time away from their already hectic schedules.

Some clients like to watch all of the auditioners. In one day, for a commercial for instance, we might see 120 actors. I doubt the client who wants to watch all of the actors we brought in is going to watch all 120 auditions. For those clients who just want to see the best, the casting office will upload and forward only a selection.

Please note that the task of selecting the best, converting the footage, editing, uploading, attaching headshots electronically, and logging the session for the client is arduous and must be done the same day or night of the session. There is no rest for the weary (casting director, associate and assistant).

Another big change in the last three years is that actors put themselves on tape more than ever. It used to be that if you were an actor who did not live in Los Angeles or New York, you had to go to your local agent's office and they would record you. Your agent would have to mail or overnight the completed VHS tape or DVD. The casting director on the other end would have to retrieve the mail, open the package, and watch every tape or DVD that would come in from all around the country. Sometimes the taped auditions were watched and sometimes they were not. You never knew if yours had been one of the lucky ones until you got a callback. You rarely if ever got feedback on the tapes you sent to the larger markets, so it felt like all the work of auditioning and sending would go into this black hole. Worse, let's say you didn't have an agent and you had to hire a videographer to shoot you. Auditioning remotely was very expensive in the past.

Nowadays, with the cost of a video or digital camera being so affordable and with the ease of use, an actor can self-tape and do so in the comfort of their own home. In fact, it's imperative now that an actor own some sort of digital camera (with a tripod) as well as have a basic knowledge of converting, editing, and uploading auditions on a computer via the Internet.

What's more, thanks to YouTube, Vimeo, YouSendIt, and the ease with which one can create and maintain their own website, it's so much less time-consuming for a casting director to watch taped auditions. We don't have to leave our desks now to watch auditions from out-of-town, and, in fact, we have the capability to watch them from any device anywhere. Plus, you are informed when we download and/or watch your tape. We are much more likely now to watch remote auditions that come our way.

Before you embark on taping your auditions and sending them in to us, however, I would strongly advise you practice first on camera. Two of the young actors I interviewed for this book, Sarah Drew and Mark J. Sullivan, both told me the best thing they did, from the moment they graduated from college, was to tape themselves on a daily basis. They would practice doing monologues or scene work in front of a camera and watch the results.

Sarah realized she needed help after her first on-camera audition, which she felt was a disaster of overindulgent emotions. She knew if she was to book jobs in

TV and film, she needed to find a way to calibrate and translate all her great theatre training for the camera. Sarah created a space in her tiny apartment in which she set-up a camera and tripod. The equipment lived there always so as to ensure she used it easily and often. She taped herself before every single audition, only saying her lines, and got many takes. Afterwards, she'd watch the footage on her TV monitor, analyzing the work with an honest, open mind. At first, she was horrified by what she saw. She felt her demeanor was too animated, "too big," and the constant movement of her eyebrows drove her crazy. But by doing and watching these auditions over and over again, on a daily basis, she learned to "calm down her expressions, calm down her brows. Basically think what (she) wanted to think and not show anything." In essence she taught herself how to make more subtle choices and "narrow the emotions into (her) eyes."

Mark confessed his frustration with his on-camera auditions at the start of his career. He feared he was too big on-camera, but then if he did less, he was worried that what he was doing wasn't coming across. It's very common for actors coming from a theatre background to be confused by how far to internalize their emotions. For fear of being "too theatrical," they end up doing nothing, or worse, having "dead eyes." The only way Mark has been able to viscerally think and feel his way beyond this confusion is to get together with a friend and tape everything. He accumulates real audition sides or transcribes scenes from movies for the material to be used. Sometimes, he just talks into the camera a la "The Office." Just as Sarah got more believable, Mark is learning to "create the scene in a very small frame." Before each practice session, he asks himself basic questions like: "Where are the other speakers in the room? How do I address them? How do I make the scene believable and interesting, while not being distracting from the actual text?" In this context, where the pressure is removed, he has the chance to better his on-camera skills and create a superior taped audition. By practicing this way, Mark has taught himself how to "let go of the performance of it."

Only when you get to the point where you feel comfortable in front of the camera and no longer cringe when watching yourself on the playback are you ready to self-tape your auditions and send them in to us.

When the time is right, here are a few practical pointers I'd advise you to follow:

1) Keep your shots simple. As with the live auditions, it's all about your eyes and making a connection with us. Don't look down at your sides too much. Some casting directors and most of the top coaches will tell you not to look directly into the camera. I've heard it said that the best way is to look at the reader, who should be right next to the camera on either side, or to hang a photo or piece of tape next to the camera and pretend that's your reader. However, I think it's best to talk to the camera as if it's your scene partner, as if you're talking to a confidante. In this way, the more you're connecting with the lens, the more we'll see your face and, most critically, your thoughts as we watch. But I think I'm in the minority in this belief.

2) Make sure the lighting accentuates your eyes and have a simple solid colored background, such as a white or pale wall. Remove any pictures or photos that might be on that wall.

3) Sit close to the mic or, better yet, use a separate clip-on mic. We need to hear you clearly, and if you're reading with a scene partner who is off camera, it's best we don't hear them as much as you.

4) Keep your "slate" as simple as possible. Slating before a taped audition is where you state your name and contact information before you start the scene. If you have representation, state your agency and agent's name. If you don't have representation, just state "direct." You don't need to tell us your phone or email information on the tape. It will be stated on your resume that you will send along with the audition.

If you're under eighteen years of age, you should state your date of birth. If you're an adult, don't tell us your age, height, or weight. Don't tell us about yourself or try to think of something cute to say. Just tell us your name, representation info, and what role you're reading for.

Just as with your audition, your slate should be as natural and relaxed as possible without being lackadaisical. It should exude a positive energy without trying too hard, and if it comes off stiff or lifeless, we won't be interested in the audition.

5) Make sure you follow the directions clearly stated by the casting director on whether to include a full body shot, profiles, and the like. Some require many shots of you and others just need a close up. The instructions will be specific, so there won't be any mystery as to what is required of you.

If you have not been requested to go on tape by either the casting director (directly) or the agent who is submitting you, then you're sending a "blind submission." Blind submissions can be a waste of time. I know some actors read online that so-and-so casting director is looking for the next action star in Bryan Singer's next film. The actor then takes the time, money and energy to find the contact information of the casting director on the Internet, create an audition tape, and forward the audition to the unsuspecting casting director. The odds of that audition being watched are a million to one. We simply don't have the time to view auditions unless they were requested by us or forwarded by an agent we trust. And the odds of that blind submission being good enough to warrant a callback are even more astronomical. But if someone can prove me wrong by booking a huge job on a blind submission, please let me know and I will stand corrected.

Callbacks

So now you might ask the obvious, "What is a good audition?" When are you most likely to get a producer's or director's callback? You'll get chosen by the casting director to move forward in the audition process when your pre-read (live or on tape) shows/reveals the following:

You're relaxed.

You're able to reveal yourself with discipline (vs. indulgence) and depth.

If it's for a role in a comedy, you're able to make us laugh by revealing your own unique sense of humor.

You're fully prepared but with the ability to come off spontaneous and fresh.

Your thought processes as the character are clear within the scene. You've done your "beat" work, where every change of thought is clearly delineated.

You're not over-rehearsed or over-coached - stuck in a "performance."

If we give you direction, you're able to implement it with ease.

We enjoy being in The Room with you (or watching you on tape).

We connect with you emotionally (vs. intellectually).

We are excited by you. You have a "wow!" factor and not just a "good" or "fine" factor. You will not get a callback if we think you're pretty good. You'll get a callback if we think you're fantastic.

You fit the role. (Or at least your performance has convinced us.)

When you do get a callback, congratulations! This is no small feat. For one normal TV co-star or guest star role, we'll most likely pre-read twenty to fifty actors and only bring five to the producers' callback. We're usually casting six to eight roles per episode for a half-hour comedy and twenty per episode for an hour show, so you do the math; we're seeing a lot of actors in a short time frame. Getting a callback is second only to actually booking the job, and you should be ecstatic to make it to the next round. You have our attention. We love you. We only bring the top auditioners to the callback as our jobs depend on the acting ability of the actors we choose.

Some actors are considered "straight to producers." They are in this category because we know them so well in The Room and are 100% confident in their ability to audition well.   Oftentimes, these actors will have booked with us before or have excelled at their pre-reads. Another reason an actor may forego the pre-read process is if a particular actor's agent insists their client doesn't pre-read. It's a prestige factor. The actor has worked consistently and so why should they have to meet with the casting director first?   This happens a lot during pilot season. I understand this way of thinking – auditions of any kind are a chore and isn't it nice to go directly to the callback without the preliminary one?

Skipping the pre-read is not always in the actor's best interest, however.   More often than not, the only direction an actor will get is with the casting director.   We know what the producers are looking for and it is only during the pre-read that we have the time and inclination to direct the actor to help them book the job.   The callback for TV is always very stressful and not the best time for direction to take place. The producers are incredibly busy folks and the casting session takes them away from the writers' room.   The producers, even the sweet ones, can't wait for the casting session to be over so they can resume writing.   Also, some are uncomfortable in the audition as they might not know how to talk to an actor.

According to Phil Rosenthal ("Everybody Loves Raymond" creator), the truth of the matter is "a television writer's main preoccupation is 'Where's lunch? Where are we going to order from today because we have a lot of work to do, so we're going to work through lunch.' Lunch is the only sunshine coming into the room." Since they do not wake up in the morning looking forward to hearing actors speak their words for the very first time in the callback audition room, it's best to meet with the casting director alone first before entering.

It is during the callback for TV that an actor really needs to nail the audition on the first take. If you've gotten a callback from a pre-read, it's imperative you recreate the final audition you had in the pre-read session, the exact audition that got you the callback in the first place. Don't go home between your pre-read and your callback and think, "Oh, how about if I add this cute line reading. I can make it funnier that way!" If your callback is substantially different from your pre-read, you'll irritate the casting director, which you want to avoid. We're helping you out. We took the time to direct you in the first place. Don't mess with a good thing. We know what we're doing, and even if some of us don't, listen to us anyway.

This is an extreme case, but I once had an actor come in to a producer's session. I had pre-read and directed him. He was difficult in The Room but a good actor who I had seen in plays at the Mark Taper Forum in Los Angeles. I wanted to give him a shot even though he was fighting me in the pre-read. He came into the callback and had the gall to say to the producers, "I don't agree with the direction I was given by the casting director and so I'd like to try it my own way." The actor not only embarrassed me in front of my boss, but he came off as difficult and argumentative, two traits not highly regarded in actors.

As always, be a perfect human being in the callback. Be brilliant and keep the casting director happy.

The callback for film, which is with the director and not the producer, is considerably less stressful than for TV. You're meeting with the director so you will be directed, which is a gift. For TV, you're auditioning for the next episode while the producers are shooting the current one. This situation is very distracting for them. The atmosphere is frenetic. For film, it's only about that particular movie, and so the pace is leisurely in comparison. Unless you're auditioning for a series regular, the producers in TV don't have time to get to know you as a person separate from your audition. In film, the director wants to get to know you. He will chat with you before the audition begins. He might ask you questions about the role. He might tell you that you can veer from the script and improvise if you feel inclined. This will hardly ever happen in TV.

No matter what room you're in, whether it's for a TV show or a studio film, go with the flow of the room and let the casting director be your guide.

You will book the job if and only if the producer or the director is excited by you and if you're a great fit for the role. You don't have to be what they initially imagined for the role. You don't have to fit the character description in either the breakdown or the script, you just have to fit the role in The Room. You have to own that role. The actor who will book a particular role is so committed to that part that he's not going to let anyone else have it, or so it seems. There is energy, passion, and a sense of spontaneity to the audition. The actor has abandoned himself to the role. There is no self-consciousness to the audition. We, the casting director and either the producer or director, just sit back and enjoy. There is a depth, command, and sense of either joy or sadness, depending on the genre, to the audition.

As with the pre-reads, you will be video taped during the callback. Thanks to the new technology, it's so easy for, let's say, the Director of Casting at CBS to watch the auditions online. Whereas previously we might have faxed over the headshot and resume of the actor we wanted to hire for a guest spot, it's now the standard for the networks and studios to approve of nearly every role that is cast on a TV series by watching the digital uploads.

The same is true with films, commercials, even webseries. The "client" such as *Nike* or *Subway* (both of which I've worked for on webseries) must always approve of an actor before we can hire him or her. By "client" I mean a whole team of people that includes the Head of Marketing, the creatives, and even the CEO in some cases. The folks in positions of power must watch the auditions, and thanks to the new technology, they don't have to travel around the country anymore to do so.

chapter two

What Is Good Acting?

Although this is not a book on acting technique, it's a book on how to audition well, I feel compelled to bring up the subject of good acting and how I can assess an actor's ability in The Room in a matter of seconds.

Some great actors have had substantial training and some have not. I am biased toward the well-trained theatre actor because I am passionate about theatre and the special devotion it takes to pursue that love. Oddly, there doesn't seem to be a correlation between success as a working actor and training. Mark Duplass ("The League," *Your Sister's Sister*) has never had a formal acting class in his life. As long as you're a good, compelling actor, you will book jobs. Actors who graduate from Julliard (Jessica Chastain) book jobs and actors who have never had an acting class in their life work regularly in both TV and film.

I'm fascinated by the intangibles of acting. Whenever I'm emotionally moved by a performer, either on a screen or on a stage, I wonder what is it about this actor that I'm so drawn to? And as an actor, you have to find a way to translate what you know intellectually into your physical and emotional self. For most actors, this will mean being committed to the study of acting in a class and/or performing in plays. Taking classes and working on the stage will not guarantee you will book jobs in TV and film, however. Being a good, compelling actor in The Room will.

So what is good acting in The Room?

Good acting is non-acting acting. We, the audience and especially the casting director and the director/producer, don't want to see the work. We don't want to see you "act." The transition from you as a person to you as the character should be seamless. When you say your lines, it should seem as if you were having a private intimate conversation, with the casting director as the voyeur.   There should be no artifice or veneer to the dialogue.

Good acting is from your gut and your heart, not from your head. Good acting is your ability to reveal many emotions simultaneously in a made-up situation - the "Magic If" in Stanislavski terms. If I were a teenaged girl who sought escape in drugs (the film Thirteen), how would I feel in this situation? What emotional qualities would I bring to this role? True and deep emotions play well in The Room.

A good actor is relatable, likable, natural, and fully connected to the other person. A good actor listens and reacts in the moment to what is going on in the scene.   If you're too self-conscious to go to an intimate place, where you really and truly connect with another human being, you will not audition well. If you're uncomfortable with intimacy in The Room – if you continually "check out" of the scene when it starts getting good and connected – you will not book work.

Finally, good acting draws us in as if there were a magnetic force field surrounding the actor. It's imperative you find your force field. A good actor is a charismatic person.

How can you enhance your *charisma* in The Room? Read on.

How Can You Stand Out?

How do you stand out from the hordes of other actors vying for the same role? The answer is not what you would think. It's not that you have to come in and be "different" or "make a bold choice" to wake the casting director up from the stupor of having to hear the same material over and over again. "Standing out from the crowd" does not mean using an accent when none is called for or wearing a silly hat. Standing out does not come from the outside but from within. That's one reason it makes me nervous when some acting teachers tell actors to "make bold choices." If you're thinking about how you can be different, your focus is in the wrong place.

You can't obsess over the other actors coming in for the same role either. More often than not you'll be sitting in the waiting area with actors you recognize from TV shows and automatically think they'll get the job over you because they have better resumes than yours or they are better actors than you are. We don't want you to try to be more like them. We're not looking for an "image." As Alex Loyd says in his terrific self-help book, *The Healing Code* (www.thehealingcode.com), the erroneous precept that "image is everything" originates from the belief that "I'm not okay, and if people get to know me, they will come to that same conclusion, so whatever the cost I need people to see a manufactured me instead of who I really am." Portraying yourself in an inauthentic, pre-packaged way is manipulation in the worst way and we can see right through that.

In truth, you can wow us by simply being yourself. This is true in all auditioning, but especially for TV roles. All we want is you, and to see your authentic, natural charisma coming through the character.

Casting directors are like matchmakers between the director, producer, creator, and the actors. Metaphorically, I ask myself, would I want to date this person? Or just have coffee and look for an excuse to leave? Would I consider a long-term relationship? Marriage? The auditioner who gets the "marriage proposal" is the one who gets the job.

What do we look for? What makes us want to watch a particular actor over another? *Charisma.* Charisma is the bedrock of how we connect with each other as human beings. It's the foundation of how we communicate with each other. Without charisma, without sex appeal, without attraction, without the force and chemistry between people, our lives would be dull and boring as hell. Without charisma, your audition will put us to sleep.

I've come to realize, because of all the hours I've spent in that room, that the key ingredients to the Art of Charisma are **self-knowledge** and **balance**. In order to tap into the full power of your individual charisma, you absolutely must know who you are and then have the ability to reveal that true self in The Room. If you aren't brave enough to look deep within in order to truly know and accept who you are, then you most likely won't be a very good actor.

Your true self is a reflection of both your dark and light qualities. A charismatic person is the perfect balance of the two. If you are all dark qualities, you will scare us, and if you are all light qualities, we won't be emotionally moved by you. Shakespeare's plays are all about self-knowledge and balance. If you're too much of one thing, you either end up dead or your family is destroyed (*Macbeth, King Lear*). If you're the perfect balance of man and woman, dark and light, you end up happily married (Rosalind in *As You Like It*).

So you must ask yourself, with honesty and fearlessness, "Who am I? What emotional qualities do I possess?" As an actor, the only thing you can play is emotions. It's the only thing the audience responds to, really. You think we're attracted to hot bodies? No. We're attracted to a strong emotional inner life. Adele won a gaggle of Grammys in 2012 for writing and singing songs that are extremely emotional. Apparently, whether we listen to very happy songs or very sad songs, dopamine is released when we feel and either way we are elated by this. Feeling makes us feel better.

In embarking on your journey of self-knowledge, try this simple exercise. Make a list of who you are emotionally. What are your emotional qualities? How would you describe yourself in one-word descriptions - sad, angry, optimistic, caring, fierce, funny, smart, passionate? Your list should be at least ten qualities long, although fifteen to twenty is best. You should be brutally honest. Who are you really? Are you depressed, melancholy, joyous? Are you skeptical, laid back, romantic? You can have contradictory traits and, in fact, it's best if you do. You can be loving and difficult, angry and peaceful. A complex person is an interesting person. An interesting actor succeeds in The Room.

Your list of qualities might look like this:

DARK	LIGHT
Angry	Passionate
Frustrated	Joyous
Sad	Funny
Insecure	Sexy
Bitter	Brave
Fearful	Optimistic

Most people only show one or two of their qualities to folks they're meeting for the first time. The above list I made for myself. I probably only show smart and funny to strangers. I might show four or five qualities (smart, funny, optimistic, brave) to my close friends and six or seven (add in angry and sad) to my mate. When I'm alone in my private space I reveal all of my qualities, especially those I want to hide (bitter, insecure, fearful). Sadly, most people are not expressing to others the full gamut of their emotional lives. My darker qualities are not easy to take but they do make up who I am. They are part of my emotional arsenal. If I'm not expressing my authentic self to the world, I'm gypping my colleagues, friends, and family of connecting with me on a deep and meaningful level. Most people are definitely in this group with me.

Actors are not most people. It is your job to connect with other human beings. It's your obligation to know yourself and have the courage to reveal at least five of your qualities in every audition, every scene, every Room.   If you're too nervous to reveal yourself the second you walk in the The Room, you won't get the role. If you're uncomfortable in your own skin, you won't let us in. You need to let us in. We need to see you.   You can't be protective of your emotions, especially the darker ones.

The tricky part is that you need to reveal your authentic self the moment we come in contact with you. You can't come in inauthentic or emotionally blocked and then maybe five minutes into the audition, we finally start seeing a glimmer of who you are.   There is no "warming up" in The Room.

That is not to say that if you're an angry person, you should come in showing your anger, or if your depressed, you should come in wallowing in your angst. You should come in The Room in a good place, but then emotionally available to us and what is required in the scene.

A great audition contains at least five emotional qualities. You can grab what you can from your own personal arsenal and choose what is appropriate for the particular role. For instance, if you're auditioning for a role on "Law and Order: SVU," you might choose from the list above funny, angry, passionate, brave, and sad. If your audition is one note, one emotion, such as sadness, it will be boring. If it's just bitter, it will be indulgent. Human nature is multifaceted, so should your auditions be.

The list you've made of your own emotional qualities is a beautiful tool you can refer to always, even as you revise it. You can go to your darker qualities for the dramatic scenes and the lighter ones for the comedic. You can combine your dark and light qualities for the leading roles in either genre. You can go to your lightest of the light qualities for commercial auditions.

You don't have to bring in anything to the audition that is foreign to you. You don't need to conjure up emotions that you've never experienced. It's all you and it will work for any scene, any role, in all media.

chapter three

My Top Ten Secrets of Charisma

In addition to advising you to gain self-knowledge and balance, I'd now like to offer you my Top Ten Secrets of Charisma to help enhance your chances of succeeding in The Room. These tips were formulated after watching way too many actors blow their chances. They also come from observing brilliance. They are lessons learned from the inner sanctum of booking jobs in TV and film.

1: Reveal Your 'Natural Sexiness'

Come on, let's face it, there is nothing like looking into your lover's face and seeing his or her eyes look at you in "that way." The eyes are open, relaxed, and thinking only about you in a lovely way. They have a positive energy – a desire - and you can't help but be drawn in. The person who looks at you in that moment is sexy, and casting directors are drawn to this natural sexiness as well. We are human, after all. We love actors partly because they are sexy. Sexiness is the basis of what makes people attracted to each other in the first place. If you can somehow convey your natural sexiness without being overtly flirty - or trying too hard and coming on too strong - you immediately have us in your corner. If you can walk into The Room and look us in the eyes, feeling good, positive, and sexy, we will be excited to experience your audition.

To clarify this point, I am not suggesting that you come on to the casting director. I'm not promoting that you dress in a trashy fashion (unless it's called for in the scene, of course), say anything in a provocative manner, or enter expecting to experience the "casting couch" in order to get the role. I am not talking about sexiness in a disrespectful or uncomfortable way. I am talking about one's own innate sexiness that is reflected in the eyes and in attitude and confidence level. In essence, I'm talking here about what is at the very core of one's charisma. Are you open as a person? Are you accessible? Do you have a natural sex appeal? The more you feel good about yourself, the more your natural sexiness will be revealed to us. That is what we want to see.

What is sex appeal? The French call it having "le chien," which literally translates to "the dog." Sex appeal is something visceral and earthy. It is not really about physical beauty. Look at Philip Seymour Hoffman. He's not the most handsome man in The Room, but on film and on stage, we can't keep our eyes off of him. What about Judi Dench, Jeanne Moreau, Angelica Houston, Gene Hackman, Paul Giamatti, Frances McDormand, to name only a few? These actors possess a life force. George Bernard Shaw's heroines possess a life force, which he described as "energy and success, the ideal of the human species." Actors who have sex appeal are the ideals in our society. We idolize them. We pay money to watch them and to read about them!

Actors we idolize embody all that life has to offer – joy, sadness, fear, disappointment, strength, vulnerability – and sometimes they can show this is one look! Russell Crowe comes on screen and we see a whole life in his eyes – which makes him sexy as hell. Kate Winslet does this also. She's gorgeous, yes, but her eyes convey the full gamut of human emotion. She has depth, and nothing could be sexier on screen.

Sexiness is being self-aware not self-conscious. Sexiness is being comfortable in your own skin. Sexiness is being open and honest about your dark side as well as your lighter one.

Actress with Dead Eyes. Nothing is going on except fear of the audition

Actress expressing her natural sexiness. Her eyes are open, revealing.

Actor with Dead Eyes. Not sexy.

Actor with relaxed, open eyes. He's accessible - sexy.

2: Create Chemistry by Making It About The Other Person

Going back to our dating metaphor, don't be a selfish lover. The scene is not all about you or your character. As in all good scenes, either on stage or on camera, it's about two people connecting through their desire. It is the chemistry between people that makes us want to watch them. What is your relationship to that other person? How do you feel about them? What do you want from them?

If you're acting by yourself we will not be drawn to you. You must connect emotionally with the other person. You must see them. You must listen and react to what they're saying to you. You must have a real give-and-take conversation with them. You must honestly talk to them as opposed to acting at them. You must be present in the moment and interested in them. This is what good acting is all about - revealing real human behavior in an unreal situation.

Sometimes you will be auditioning for co-star roles. You will come in for the Waiter, the Cop, or the Receptionist. This is the most obvious example, but in these scenes, it is definitely not about you or your character. In a comedy especially, you will be the set-up for the joke that the star will deliver. During the audition, if you make the scene all about the waiter or the cop, you will overact and tank. You will stop listening. You will try your hardest to be "Funny" (with Jazz Hands). You will want to make an impression because you will only have three to five lines in the scene. You will want to make the role bigger and more important that it is. But, the co-star role is already important. It is helping further the story. The producers, who always want to save money, are paying you a salary to play that role that pushes the story forward. But keep it real. Just listen, just talk, and know it's all about the star of the show or movie, not about the funny waiter.

Actress trying too hard to be funny. Pushing the comedy. Doesn't look natural.

Actress as herself. Good, positive energy. We want to be in The Room with her.

3: Express Vulnerability

The more we see your vulnerability, your humanness, and your reflection of the human condition, the more we are drawn to you. This is true for comic roles. This is true for dramatic roles. And, it is most effective in roles that are unsympathetic – the asshole, the bitch, the villain. If you can find the humanity in these roles, the vulnerability, your audition will have dimension, a "real life" quality, and a likeability that will make us want to watch you. If you play the unsympathetic roles on the nose, as a stereotype, we will be bored at the very least and repelled at the worst.

The nicest, most vulnerable actors make the best villains (Alan Rickman in the original *Die Hard* and in the Harry Potter series. Christophe Waltz in *Inglourious Basterds*). Sweethearts make the best bitches (Rachel McAdams in *Mean Girls*, Megan Mullally in "Will and Grace"). If an actual Karen had played the role of 'Karen' in "Will and Grace," the role would be unwatchable. That character is a drunken, sarcastic, vindictive, and hateful bitch. As played by Megan Mullally, who is one of the sweetest, most grateful actresses in the world, we love her. She played 'Karen' as completely vulnerable.

Amy Pietz ("The Office"), who is an actress with incredible pathos and vulnerability, can play - as she puts it - the most popular character-type written for actresses in their 30s, that of the "bitchy, conniving, bitter woman." All she has to do is reflect on the times in her own life when she is "bitchy," and as she so eloquently puts it, those are the times when she is fearful of something. In real life, if she is scared of something, those are the times she will lash out or "bite." When she is asked to play this kind of role, she asks of the character, "what is she the most afraid of?" which will undoubtedly lead her to the vulnerable mushy core of any strident role. This is exactly what Meryl Streep did in *The Devil Wears Prada*, playing what could have been a caricature. The scene in which we see her without her hair coiffed and with no makeup, we see how incredibly fearful and sad she really is, underneath the veneer.

Antihero roles, with increased moral complexity, such as those played by Jon Hamm ("Mad Men"), Bryan Cranston ("Breaking Bad"), Michael C. Hall ("Dexter"), Edie Falco ("Nurse Jackie"), and Mary-Louise Parker ("Weeds"), are absolutely driven by the actor's own vulnerability and innate humanity.

If you allow your vulnerability to show in the sympathetic roles – the lover, the victim, the innocent girl-next-door – not only will you book the job, you will become a beloved star, such as Amy Adams, Scarlett Johansson, Reese Witherspoon, Michelle Williams, and Ryan Gosling.

Don't be afraid to show us the side of you that only you show yourself. We all have one public persona and another that we share with our family and friends. The vulnerable you is the real persona, the person you are when you're alone at night in your personal space, stripped of any pretense. That's what we want to see. You stripped. That's why we go to the movies. That's why I found great solace and escape as a lonely teenager who had just lost her dad. I could stare up at a screen, watching actors reveal to me what I was feeling. It was far too scary a place for me to go by myself. But watching actors go there I could feel safe and was comforted.

Brilliant actors are brave folks. They go emotionally where we are scared to go. They speak from the gut. They are not afraid to show the ugly side of humanity, as long as it's real and truthful. They are raw. Ryan Gosling in everything he does is an example. So are Jeremy Renner (*The Hurt Locker, The Town*), Michael Fassbender (*Shame, Jane Eyre*), Amy Ryan (*Gone, Baby Gone*) and of course, Natalie Portman in *Black Swan*. Tommy Lee Jones in *In The Valley of Elah* is another. Jones' sorrow, disappointment, fear, terror, loneliness, strength, and disgust when he learns of his son's secret life and subsequent brutal murder are all revealed silently in his eyes and face. Judi Dench is not afraid to be vulnerable and unappealing. She is astounding in *Notes On a Scandal*. Physically, she is dowdy and old. She wears no make-up, her hair is cropped short, and she plays a woman who is monstrous. But damn: she is riveting and gorgeous in all her emotional nakedness! Her performance helps me better understand the human condition. I see a side of myself in her; a side that I don't want to admit is there. This is the kind of acting – authentic, audacious, and raw – that makes me physically shake.

These are the performances that earn Academy Award nominations.

How can an actor possibly reveal the human condition in The Room? Granted, this is a gargantuan task – but you simply must bring your full emotional life into The Room. When you audition for episodic dramas and dramatic films, you must go dark and deep with the full gamut of human emotion - pain, loss, fear, disappointment, melancholy, passion, and fierceness. These auditions can't be one or even two notes. They have to be as dynamic as possible. As I stated previously in this chapter, a great audition will be one in which you show at least five different emotions. To make matters even more difficult for you, you can't fake or push the emotions. You can't act sad. You have to be sad. We have to see it and feel it in your eyes. These auditions are very intimate and The Room is the least intimate and inviting environment there is. You have to come in and immediately "give it all you've got." There is no time to warm up within your audition. You must already be there, at that revealing, intimate place.

Actor expressing vulnerability. He draws us in.

Actress expressing vulnerability through her eyes. She has many emotions going on at one time.

4: Control The Adrenaline Rush

If you are a person who prays, I would suggest you don't ask for fame, fortune, or even just an acting job. Pray for the ability to be relaxed and centered. If you can master these two issues, everything else you need to succeed will follow.

You will not have a good audition if you're nervous. No one hires someone who is nervous. It is your job to make us comfortable and relaxed. It is your job to entertain us. A great audition happens when we simply sit back and enjoy watching you. If you're nervous, we will feel sorry for you, we will feel compassion toward you, but we will not feel comfortable hiring you and sending you to a sound stage.

A sound stage is an intimidating place. Often the director does not have time to work with you, especially in episodic television, and you will be directed only by the casting director in the audition. The director is worried about the lights, the set, the shot, the story, and a million other things. The actor who is hired must be able to handle himself on the set because if you turn out to be the problem, you will be replaced.

If you're nervous, you will not be able to take direction in The Room. If you can't take direction from the casting director and make an adjustment, then you won't get called back.

If you're tight, nervous, or blocked when you come in The Room, you will only be able to do the scene one way, your way, the way you rehearsed it. Casting directors – not you or another actor – know what will book the job. We will guide you with great knowledge and expertise because we have been doing this a long time and we want you to do well. We are on your side. We want this role to be cast and we want it to be you. If you're nervous and/or resisting the direction, you will lose our interest instantly, and once you lose that, it's hard to get called back in for anything. You have just wasted our time and time is of the essence in casting.

Especially casting for TV. Every moment counts, and if you've wasted your precious moment in a casting director's office being nervous, you will regret that for a long time.

If you find yourself in this situation – fighting or resisting the direction, not being able to hear and process the notes quickly and intelligently – try to calm down and listen. Do not think, "Damn, I'm messing up – why can't I get this?" Getting direction is a good thing, not a bad thing. If the casting director did not think you were worth it, he or she would not spend the extra time with you. Remember that when you find yourself tightening up.

There are various things you can do to help with nerves before you get in The Room. You're going in (hopefully!) for roles on the TV shows you love and in for directors whom you admire. Naturally you're going be nervous. If you're lucky enough to test for a primetime network pilot, you know going in how much money you will be making if you book it. Your life and lifestyle will literally change overnight for the better, and it's easy to lose your focus. I've seen great actors tank in these rooms due to nerves. I've had the heartbreaking experience of watching these great actors with good, strong credits start pushing the comedy when they feel the enormous pressure. What was loose and fun and hilarious in the first audition room now evolves into an audition that is fake and forced, all due to nerves. No matter how good they were in the first auditions, if they can't perform under pressure – when the stakes are very high, in front of the TV executives – they will not get hired.

Instead of taking Zanex to calm your nerves, as so many actors are prone to do, my suggestion would be to pray for help first and then do the following activities.

Hypnotherapy. This is sort of like accelerated psychoanalysis. Hypnotherapy is great for stage fright, smoking too much, drinking too much, and eating too much - pretty much anything that ails you. I live by it and can tell you firsthand it changed my life. You have to be able to abandon yourself to the Hypnotherapist; if you can do this, you will see results right away.

Stephanie Jones, a prominent HypnoTherapist, writes on her website (www.stephanie-jones.com):

Hypnosis is a natural state where the critical factor is bypassed, usually through relaxation. This allows healing, pleasing suggestions to be accepted by the subconscious mind, resulting in life-altering, permanent change.

It is a well-known fact that we come to believe and therefore achieve whatever we repeat to ourselves, whether the beliefs are true or false. The subconscious mind cannot tell the difference between a fear-based lie or a joy-filled truth. People become who they are because of their dominant thoughts, the thoughts and beliefs they hold in their subconscious mind. Thoughts become things and events in our lives.

Using the imagination and focused concentration with a hypnotic guide, you can access the beliefs and idea patterns that are held in your subconscious and alter them. Change those thoughts and beliefs to represent your authentic deeper self. Free yourself from any obsolete belief systems inherited from worn-out voices from the past.

Remember, the subconscious is the single most powerful goal-achieving mechanism known to humankind. Hypnosis allows you to access and reinforce what you want and need on a deep level and therefore manifest it in your life with greater ease.

Meditation. The practice of meditation can be an effective way for actors to combat issues with nerves as well as self-doubt. There was a time, not long ago, when meditation was considered a rarified form of enlightenment, only for gurus, "new age" participants, and those individuals who had hours on end to tune out the outer world and look inward. Not so now, as it's become commonplace for people of all walks of life and all socio-economic backgrounds to learn the principals of meditating. Classes are available now in every city and in every price range.

Meditation has many benefits, including emptying your mind of all the "noise" (inner voices that can be negative), slowing down your nervous heart rate, relaxing your body and face, and centering and focusing your energy. After meditation, the mind is sharper with enhanced creativity and memory. In fact, modern scientific research confirms that regular mediation produces a higher level of happiness and a longer life span.

The following is a simple breathing exercise that can be done before an audition, either at home or in the waiting room:

Close your eyes and inhale through your nose for a count of eight or ten.

Hold your breath for an equal time.

Exhale through the nose for a count of eight or ten.

Repeat above steps three to six times.

You can also do a "mental scanning" of your body with the following simple exercise:

Close your eyes and visualize your feet.

Inhale, imagining space and openness entering them with each inhalation.

Hold your breath for three seconds.

Exhale, feeling the tension flow out and then the heaviness or warmth remaining.

Now do the rest of the body. Inhale space and openness, and exhale tension. Each exhale of a body part should feel heavy or warm. First, do your ankles and legs, then pelvis and torso, next upper arms, forearms, wrists, and hands. Finally, shoulders, neck, throat, and head.

Open your eyes and cherish the feeling of calm that envelopes your whole body and mind.

Yoga. Practicing yoga (or meditation) on a regular basis can do wonders in helping you center yourself as a person. Centering means grounding yourself, which in turn makes you feel more alive and fully present in the moment. The more grounded you are, the better your audition will be.

The many benefits of practicing yoga on a regular basis are now common knowledge; more balanced mood, better focus on difficult tasks, improved energy and sleep, a calmer and quieter mind, and increased fitness level, all leading to being a more relaxed person. If you're not relaxed in The Room, you will not be able to reveal your true inner self, which is explained fully in the next section.

5: All We Want Is You

Casting directors don't care how cute or handsome you are, or who you know who knows so-and-so. If we can't connect with you as a person, we won't be interested in you as an actor. If you enter The Room as a different person than the one you show us in the actual scene, I guarantee we will be more interested in the one who entered first. That is all we want, the authentic you in the scene saying the dialogue as you in the situation specified in the script. It helps if you're a good person to begin with.

If you have a chip on your shoulder and you're in a negative personal zone, we will sense that right away and turn off to you. As discussed previously, if you're nervous and emotionally blocked, you won't be able to take direction. You – the real you – must remain relaxed, malleable, and easy to work with. Again, let's go back to the dating metaphor: Do you want to marry someone who's not genuine? Emotionally blocked? Afraid to reveal themselves? Heck no.

Nothing going on. Actor is emotionally closed off.

Actor trying too hard to be funny. Looks like a caricature rather than a natural character. Not genuine.

Actor just being himself. This is what we want.

6: Be A Good Listener

You've heard it a million times, but I might as well remind you: acting is reacting and good acting is listening. Film or TV acting is not about you pontificating or talking into the air, it is about you listening to what the other person has to say as if for the first time. We then need to see the reaction register on your face and specifically in your eyes, and then we need to hear the line or reaction. It happens in a nanosecond. But without seeing how the other person's words affect you, the scene will have no life to it. It will just be you regurgitating your lines at the proper times.

We need to hear the cue, see the reaction, and feel the response.

Beware of overreacting. You can't act the reaction. You have to think it. If you're truly present, in the moment and listening, then your reaction will be natural and beautiful. It is the reaction that moves us. We want to see how you're affected. It is in that spark that magic happens.

The last thing we want to see is you acting. Good on-camera acting is non-acting acting. If you're acting, we will want to flee from The Room. We just want the real you, talking to us. That's all the scene usually is, just two (or perhaps a few more) people talking to each other. We want you to talk to us, not act as if you're the only one working in The Room. It's not "work." It's just a conversation.

7: Show Humility

You hear of cocky actors who take advantage of their fame. You hear of stuck-up actresses who obsess about their looks and complain about their weight and age. Don't be one of these. In your darker moments, you imagine that the actor with the largest ego, who is the most arrogant, gets the job. Believe me, he doesn't. Especially as a young actor who is just making the audition rounds, you must not allow yourself to try masking insecurity with cockiness. Just like in dating, that is one of the biggest turn-offs there is. Be confident, not arrogant. There is a huge difference. Confidence is having a sure sense of yourself; feeling comfortable in your own skin. Arrogance is when you do not feel sure of yourself but you act as if you do.

David Hyde Pierce, to me, is the epitome of the humble actor. Not only is he an excellent actor, he is also one of the most gracious, generous, humble person I met in all of my travels. He is saintly, in fact, and grateful for all the good fortune that has come his way. To me, he is the ideal actor and ideal human being, and if all of us could be like him, the world would be a better place.

It is true, alas, that there are a lot of cocky actors and actresses out in the world. But the truly humble and gracious actors will get the lasting attention of the casting directors.

If you're not feeling secure with yourself, take classes, go into therapy, do anything, but don't carry the baggage that you're "all that" into The Room.

On the other end of the spectrum, there are very good actors who don't want to come off as cocky, so they err by being so humble that they make themselves invisible. Their inner dialogue is one of "I don't want to be a needy actor so I will act as if I don't need the casting director at all." In this case, the actor comes off as apathetic or, worse, aloof. Trying to make yourself invisible is just as arrogant as trying to make yourself more important than you are. It is putting on a façade that prevents us from seeing who you really are and the façade is just a mask for deep insecurity.

8: Don't Think So Much

There is nothing that kills an audition faster than actors analyzing their work as they're doing it. Good acting does not come from your intellect; it comes from your gut. It's great to prep a scene and understand what it's about, what you want in the scene, what is your subtext, your back story, etc. But when you actually audition in The Room, the scene must be done as if you're saying those words in that situation with that other person for the first time. There has to be spontaneity to the scene, otherwise it will be too studied – too rehearsed. It will not have a life of its own.

Also, and more importantly, if, as you're doing the scene, you're having an inner dialogue – "God, I blew that line," "Damn, it went better as I was doing it on the drive over here," "How come I'm not connected?" – you will kill your chance of booking the job. Just like the camera lens, we see it all. We see when you drop out of the scene. We can tell when you're not fully present in the moment. We can tell when you don't even believe in what you're saying. When you're self-conscious.

I'm not saying you shouldn't prepare a scene. In fact, it's only when you have prepared a scene fully that you get out of your head. And I don't mean memorize the lines on the page or analyze it until you've taken all the life out of it. It's not that mechanical. You have to work on the audition scene until it is fully in your bones, until you begin feeling emotions within the scene, and until it seems like a normal conversation with normal reactions. Acting a scene will most definitely kill an audition. We don't want to see the wheels turning.

Your head has to get out of the way during your audition. You have to abandon yourself to the scene, because only then can you fly.

9: Don't Try So Hard To Be A Leader

This precept pretty much relates to everything in your life. Try too hard and you will just get tired. I learned the hard way that working harder does not mean you will automatically get the job or make more money. Many thought of me as the hardest working casting director in Los Angeles. I always took this to be a good thing. I worked 24/7, was always there for my producers no matter what the time of day, always there for the actors, seeing theatre and running workshops on my nights and weekends. I did have a great reputation, but I burned out. My life became unbalanced and I became unhealthy.

It's possible to work too hard, and, as it relates to auditioning, if your audition looks like you're working too hard, you will not get the job. Your audition should appear easy. Great athletes make their work seem easy. Great speakers, politicians, and lawyers make what they do seem easy, as if they're in full and complete command of the situation. Your job as an actor is to allow the words, the emotion, and the humor to just pour out of you naturally, as if you're in a normal conversation. You must do this whether the scene is comic or highly dramatic, even if you have to cry in the scene. You cannot appear indulgent or straining for the emotion in any way. Your audition has to appear organic, natural, as if you're truly in that moment with those feelings, as if it would appear in real life. Acting is nothing but a slice of real behavior. It cannot appear as acting; it has to appear as real. This advice applies to starring as well as smaller co-starring roles.

Casting directors use the expression "small-role fever" to describe what afflicts actors coming in for co-star roles who are trying too hard to make a big impression. A good example of small-role fever is the actor who comes in for the cop role dressed in full cop regalia: uniform, badge and (fake) gun. Some stereotype the character, using a New York accent when it's not called for, just to appear more cop-like. Unless it's to play a cop in a "Saturday Night Live" sketch, cops are real people and when we want a cop in a TV show or a film, it's usually to portray a real cop. Just be yourself. All we want is you in that situation as if it were really happening.

An actor needs to take classes, see lots of theatre and movies, and watch a lot of TV. You must exercise religiously, do yoga, and be well groomed. You must constantly work on yourself: you are your commodity. But don't work yourself into the ground and make yourself unbalanced. This brings me to the final tip. . .

10: Be Healthy Emotionally And Physically

Let's be honest here. Most of us who go into the performing arts are one or more of the following:
- very emotional (it's what makes an actor very good and can drive the layman insane);
- grew up in a dysfunctional family;
- like to party;
- are trying to compensate for something pretty huge that has been missing since childhood;
- were ridiculed as a kid;
- want to succeed at all costs.

The entertainment business is a selfish lover. It requires all of you. The hard fact is you must put it above all else, especially when you're starting out. It must come before family, before lovers, and before you. And, putting it above you is where the trouble can begin.

In order to be around for the long haul, you must be healthy in every way. If you have not been in therapy, start immediately. If you drink too much or take drugs, stop right now. If your methods of dealing with the stress of the business are destructive and escapist, find better ways to cope. If you have crippling insecurity (and believe me, most of us do), start hypnotherapy today. If you're going out after the shows every single night and partying, try to go out just three times a week. If curtailing your partying is too difficult for you, go to therapy for that. Don't use the excuse you can't afford therapy. If you can't afford it, then you probably can't afford pursuing your dreams.

Go into rehab if you have to. That's what Phillip Seymour Hoffman did when he graduated from NYU. He knew he was an addict all through college and is now vocal about it. He is a smart, responsible actor. Don't be stubborn. Don't ignore the signposts along the way that scream at you to change your ways or self-destruct.

Eat right. Exercise regularly. All the precepts that doctors have been prescribing for years? Do all of them. The ideal actor is an ideal person. You are the representative of humanity. All walks of life look up to you. They all want to be you. Despite the fact that government money for the arts is not there in abundance, all of society admires you, is entertained by you, would not be able to function without theatre, film, TV, webcasts, videos, and musical performances. Life would be a dull place indeed without you. You have a responsibility toward yourself, your fellow actors, and all of mankind.

A casting director can tell the moment you walk in the door whether you're abusing alcohol or drugs. Addictions permeate our society. It is so widely accepted, promoted, or ignored that self-destruction is too common. Don't destroy yourself. If you're an addict of any kind, you will destroy yourself when you make a lot of money. Money magnifies who you are at your core. If you're a good person at your core, then money will make you better. If you're an ill person at your core, then money will kill you.

Talking With . . .Amy Pietz

Amy's many TV credits include series regular roles on: "Caroline in The City" (SAG Award nomination), "Aliens in America ," "The Amazing Mrs. Novak" (title role), "Rodney," "The Weber Show," and "Muscle." Recurring: "The Office," "Trust Me," and "Ally McBeal." Telefilms: Call for Help and All Lies End in Murder. Guest Star roles include: "Curb Your Enthusiasm," "The Closer," "Nip/Tuck," "Medium," "Bones," "Burn Notice," "Law and Order, SVU," "ER," and "CSI". Amy recently starred as Chloe King's single mother in the sci-fi thriller, "The Nine Lives of Chloe King" for ABC Family. Film credits: Rudy, Jingle All The Way, Dysenchanted, Jell-Ohh Lady (which she also produced), The Whole Ten Yards, Reunion , and You. She is a graduate of the former Goodman School of Drama, which awarded her with "Excellence in the Arts" for her work in radio, television and theatre, and has extensive credits on the stage, some of which are: A View From The Bridge and You Can't Take It With You (Steppenwolf Theatre), A Dead Man's Apartment (Met Theatre), The Boswell Sisters (The Old Globe), Christmas In Naples (Williamstown Theatre Festival), Lobby Hero (Odyssey Theatre) (Ovation nomination), and at LA's Reprise, the musicals, Fiorello and Company (Ovation nominee -Best Featured Actress in a Musical). Amy has also done over 20 audio recordings with L.A. Theatre Works.

CR: Amy, you're such a good actress I don't know where to begin. One of the reasons I wanted to interview you specifically is that you've done it all. You've been on a series ("Carolyn In the City"). You've recurred on series ("The Office"). You came from the theatre world and you still love theatre and do theatre whenever you can. You have a well-rounded good career. And you've been in Los

Angeles for nearly 20 years. You have the career that any young actor would want to emulate.

Can you speak briefly about what are the differences between being a series regular and a recurring character. Where do you find the most balanced life?

AP: The most balanced *life* or the most balanced *career?* They are kind of the same. They feed into each other. And I think balance has to happen on a daily basis. You know, we (actors) are not blessed with a life of set routines. Because I have to do a lot of different things to keep myself going in the workplace, the tricky part is accepting the fact that I'll never know when I can take a trip for pleasure, when I can go to a graduation or a close friend's wedding or funeral. And knowing and accepting that that's the trade off for having excitement. I never know what's around the corner, and I'm often surprised by great things that happen unexpectedly. This spontaneity can also be the cause of great pain for your loved ones. You can't always be relied upon say six months in advance, or sometimes one month in advance, to attend certain important events or vacations. So that is tricky.

I'm not sure if I answered your question.

CR: Not really, but it's a better answer because part of this book is about how to be a healthy, balanced actor. And that your loved ones *do* pay a cost. An actor really needs to look at the reality of that issue.

AP: Yes! It does really allow you to reinforce every day your appreciation for this *today*.
In terms of balancing out different genres, different forms of storytelling, whether I do a film or a TV show, it's not up to me to balance it out. (It's really up to the casting gods.) I try to say "yes" to as many things as possible, and I have a very broad criteria. The first is that I have to love the character. I have to

believe that it will be a reciprocal thing. I don't do a huge amount of favors anymore.

In the past, I used to do *everything* that came my way. I used to do a lot of favors and non-paying acting jobs that I was offered. Now, I'm more selective. I have to love the person asking for the favor or if I really believe in the project. And if I think I'm going to have fun doing it, because if I'm not going to have fun, then nobody watching it will have fun.

CR: What happens when you get on a project that ends up not being fun or is vastly different than what you thought it was going to be, in a negative way? How do you keep up your enthusiasm or good energy?

AP: I form relationships within the cast and crew, so that I make it an enjoyable place to go to work to every day. I *have to* enjoy it. This is especially true on a television series where you are a regular and there might be big problems with either the material, a particular co-worker, or your boss. When I find myself in this kind of negative situation, I focus on the enjoyment I can derive from anywhere within the context of the project. Maybe I'll focus on the fact that, hey, I get to go to someplace every single day and pretend that I have a real world job, a non-Hollywood job. It might be finding enjoyment in the fact that I have a routine and I know when I'm going to exercise, when I'm going to eat, that kind of stuff. If it gets down to that, where I have to *find* something to be grateful for because the circumstances are that negative, then it's sad and becomes a real challenge. I've been in this situation before.

Not every project is fulfilling, unfortunately.

I don't think any project I've worked on has had *every single element* be perfectly enjoyable. But the trick is to find *something* about it that is pleasant. It could be connecting with the craft services person, the prop master, or another actor and that's what I'll focus on. But I also try to have fun in every mini-beat, too, and not just in the macro world. **Every encounter I have on set, I really try to *connect* with people. I try to fill my days with good connection, whether it be on camera or off. We're not talking about the *craft* per se, but some of challenges that surround the craft. For myself, I really need to create strong connections with people on the set.**

CR: Speaking about the "craft" . . .you are a theatre trained actress.

AP: Yes, I received a BFA in acting from DePaul University's Theatre School in Chicago.

CR: Then did you come to Los Angeles right out of college? Did you come to Los Angeles because you were cast in a TV show?

AP: Yes, I had a very interesting and blessed start. I was living in Chicago and working at the Steppenwolf Theatre when I auditioned for a television series long-distance. The Geddes Agency made an audition tape of me and mailed it in. This was in 1993. Things were not quite digital yet. We physically had to "record" it and put it in the mail to send it to people.

From that tape, I was flown out to Los Angeles and I did test for a pilot. I didn't get that job from that first test, however, and I returned to Chicago, ready to gear up for a second pilot season that winter. But that fall I auditioned on tape for a show on The WB. It was the very first season of The WB! The show I tested for was "Muscle, a multi-camera sitcom, for Witt-Thomas. They requested I audition for two different roles within the series because they didn't really know who I was or what I was right for. In a bold move, I chose to audition for three. So I auditioned for three different roles in this large ensemble cast by going on tape, and they ended up testing me for all three roles. [This is extremely rare and in all my experiences, never seen it happen.] **For the test, I actually wore three different costumes. One role was that of an erudite British woman, one was a lesbian anchorwoman, and one was a California granola-eating masseuse. The roles were all very**

very different and it was exciting to get flown to Los Angeles and having the unique opportunity of testing in The Room for a series three different times with my three different costumes. It was really fun and exciting, to say the least.

CR: I've never heard of that happening! Testing on one show for three different roles?

AP: I hadn't either! Or since then. It was the 90s! Life was good then . .or at least for me, coming right out of school pretty much.

So in the preparation for that test [at which time one of the creators of the series will advise and direct an actor for the big audition], Nina Wass really took me under her wing. She strongly advised me to buy certain clothes for the test and to get my eyebrows done. "You're now auditioning for Television and you need to sort of know how we do things here in Hollywood." During that whole audition process, she was incredibly helpful, instructing me on the ways to present myself as a 23 year old in this foreign land.

I booked my first series regular role from this, only my second experience at testing for a pilot.

CR: Which role did you get?

AP: The lesbian anchorwoman. So we shot the pilot and it was a lot of fun. We had a great cast [Michael Boatman, Nestor Carbonell, Alan Ruck, Michole Briana White, Shannon Kenny], and it got picked for a full season (!). Due to some wonky negotiations and politics, it didn't get picked up for a second season.

It was after that first and only season of "Muscle" that I ended up testing for "Caroline in the City." [For those of you born after 1990, "Caroline in the City" starred Lea Thompson, who was then a huge star, coming off of the *Back to the Future* film series. It ran four seasons on NBC - 1995-1999 - at the height of that network's multi-camera sitcom heyday. Amy played the kooky yet sexy best friend, 'Annie,' who was a working New York/Broadway performer.]

CR: Which is where I first saw you on TV.
So let's go back to the first series - "Muscle" - that you booked right out of school, basically. How was it going from doing theatre in Chicago to getting thrown into the Los Angeles scene on a television series as a regular?

AP: It was hugely shocking and hugely euphoric. It was very emotional because I come from a lower middle class family background. We didn't have a lot of money, so for me to achieve my dream just blew my mind. I was highly emotional about it. I felt set free. I had student loans to pay off, although I was fortunate to have gotten some scholarships to DePaul. While a student, I had to work all hours over the weekends to pay for my living expenses. To say the least, it was really hard for me just to get through college financially. For me to be able to pay off my student loans *and* see the future ahead that didn't involve waiting tables . . .well, that was my goal! And I achieved that goal, in a fairly short span of time (!).

I remember vividly, during the audition process for "Muscle," being driven around by a production assistant in a Honda Civic, from the airport to my fancy hotel where I was put up by The WB. I went to the network offices and then to the studio, as if in a dream, telling myself that as soon as I book this job, I'm going back to Chicago and burn my waitress uniform. And that's what I did!

I experienced culture shock after getting on the series. Going from the midwest to Los Angeles was really really different, but not in any of the ways I expected. Everyone in Los Angeles seemed so *nice* to me and *seemed* so enthusiastic about me and my work that I was actually mistrustful of the way I was treated. One of the biggest mistakes I made, at the beginning of my career, was mistrusting their enthusiasm. I had heard Hollywood was just so *evil* and that no one says what they mean. Oddly,it was really hard for me to choose an agent and to choose

a manager and to understand that they *did* believe in me. At the time, I didn't really think anyone really believed in me or was really supporting my career, so it was hard from me to make decisions concerning representation.

If I had actually trusted some of the people who wanted to represent me - and there were a lot of them - my career might have gone even better than it has. I mistakenly saw myself as fresh meat in a land of *sharks.* That's how I viewed them, as sharks, not because they *were* but because of the misconceptions I had heard about Los Angeles back in the midwest. The agents who were interested in me were in truth incredibly reputable and excellent at handling major stars. And they wanted to handle me, too, but because of the cultural differences, I didn't trust that. I come from a world where it's encouraged to be humble and not overachieve, for fear of coming off too big for your britches. My cultural norm at the time was to blend in and not stand out too much. And the people I met in Los Angeles were asking me to *celebrate* who I was and to really go -for-it. This went against my natural inclination and how I was culturally indoctrinated. Does this make any sense?

CR: Oh yes. I think this happens to a lot of talented young actors coming from all over the United States.

AP: If I had chosen certain other agents than I had, who knows where my career would have taken me? I chose the very conservative route and I was very protective of my soul. I was scared that I'd be taken advantage of because I wasn't used to people being so direct. I didn't trust in people who went for the gold, so I sat back a bit.

Things still turned out well. I still have a good career. But that's the one thing I do wonder about. If I had chosen differently early on, might I have been a movie star?

CR: Also, if you hadn't been so mistrustful, you might have enjoyed your early career a lot more.

AP: Yes, I was very guarded and very nervous. At times, I was totally confused about the enthusiasm displayed toward me. A lot of actors struggle because they can't get *enough* people interested, but when I first came out to Los Angeles, I had *too many* people interested. I couldn't figure out who to trust.

CR: Let's talk about *nerves* for a moment. Did you have any issues with nerves when you were testing for the pilot that first time?

AP: Yes. I have struggled with nerves my entire career. Sometimes, particularly bad. I've experienced nausea, vomiting, uncontrollable shaking, hyperventilation, and tunnel vision. I still suffer from some of these things. I had a phobia of singing even though I am a good singer. On "Caroline," I played a Broadway actress who was starring in *Cats*. The first time I had to sing on the show, I threw up in my dressing room. I was terrified to go in front of the audience. So yes, nerves have been a big obstacle to overcome in my life.

I've dealt with the issue in many different ways, mainly psychological. I try to trick myself into relaxation. In my preparation for an audition, for instance, I create an environment, in my mind, of where the *character* is. I picture the room in which the scene takes place. I visualize the color of the walls. When I'm actually doing the audition, I see the scene partner in my mind's eye instead of the face of the casting director, who is actually doing the scene with me. I concentrate so much on the image in my mind of the scene that the executives on the couches watching me don't exist anymore.

In my 30s, I was fortunate enough to hire a singing coach - Eric Vetro - who helped me considerably with my singing phobia, which in turn helped me with my nerve issues. An actor should find help any way they can because you will lose a potential job if you appear nervous. If you're too nervous, the producers will think you don't know how to do your job.

I still struggle with this, even during the current pilot season. If you really want something, the primal fight-or-flight unconscious response kicks in. I usually shake in every audition I have. I have a lot of nervous energy.

CR: I'm surprised to hear this because it hasn't stopped you from getting work.

AP: I don't know. Sometimes I'm able to cover it better. Sometimes I have to talk about it in the room. I ask if I can take a moment to get myself together. It's very humbling, being in this position.

CR: It's pilot season now. Do you still have to audition, nearly twenty years after your first pilot season?

AP: There have been times in my career where I have gotten straight offers for a series. My last job on a series - "The Nine Lives of Chloe King" - was a straight offer. During the 2011 pilot season, I had straight offers because of my recurring stint on "The Office" which invigorated my IMDB Starmeter ranking and got me a lot of renewed attention. For this current pilot season (2012), I'm finding myself having to audition a lot more. And I'm getting called in to audition on a lot of projects.

CR: Well, because you're so good for so many kinds of roles. I mean, look at your first pilot season! You were considered for three different roles for one show!

AP: Yes, there are lots of roles out there for me. Last week I auditioned for a country singer ("Nashville"). They offered Connie Britton the role [who had a particularly hot year in 2011], but she hadn't accepted yet, so the producers were looking at other women, which is usual procedure. It's a bit tricky, psychologically preparing yourself for a big audition in which you are aware that the role has already been offered to someone else, which has happened to me quite a few times. It's

a difficult situation to be in, as you can imagine. You really want and need to believe that you are the only person for the job, and obviously, someone else has a different idea. It's quite out in the open and obvious. In these circumstances, I go in the room knowing that even if they couldn't imagine a brunette doing the lead, they are creating a whole new world and there are other parts they can write and create *for* you if they really love what you do in the audition. They can bring you back for something else. You are laying seeds and a foundation for another job.

CR: You really are good for a lot of different roles. Have you ever had to "type" yourself? What are your feelings on typecasting?

AP: What I'm experiencing this pilot season is that because I can do a lot of different statuses - I can do geeky women, I can do classy women, I can do unattractive, I can do attractive - I'm finding that now that I'm in my 40s, it's getting harder for me. I imagine it might be easier if I were just one type. It would definitely be less stressful for me. Right now, I have to prepare so many different types of roles. As far as actually booking the jobs, however, I'm falling somewhere in between the cracks. I'm close but no cigar. I think that has a lot to do with the fact that I am malleable. I can't really speak about being typecast because I don't experience that myself. I don't know what it's like to be just the "curly haired fat funny guy."

CR: Were you ever just the "leading ingenue?"

AP: I've always been a character actress. In my 30s, I was considered more "leading lady," yes. But I've gone from like the "slutty best friend" to the "bitchy, conniving, bitter older woman." You're either a victim, mother of a victim, or a bitch. That's kind of it.

CR: Okay, that's funny.

Switching gears a bit, when you were first making the transition from stage actress to on-camera work, were you ever told you were "too theatrical"?

AP: Yeah, I got that a lot.

CR: How did you learn to calibrate yourself?

AP: Well, it probably took me . . ..twenty years. What can happen is swinging from being too theatrical to the other side of the pendulum which is not communicating all that you are feeling and being stirred up within you because you're too afraid of overacting. I think it's about focusing all that energy and all the preparation you've done and all the choices you've made. Focusing it behind the eyes, as opposed to in the theatre, where you use your whole body. On the other hand, sometimes you need to use your whole body so it can be behind the eyes. It's tricky. It depends on what the shot is. If it's a close up, you have to keep it behind the eyes. For a wide shot, you have to involve your whole body, and let it flow through you. It's about *energy control*. It's not about making any different choices.

I used to get comments on my vocal projection. That was the first dead give away that I had come from theatre. Comments I received were that I was too loud and too articulate. But for the more emotional choices, you can hide them too much. My advise to actors going from theatre to on-camera work is to breathe and to let the energy flow freely through you. Whenever there is a blockage of energy, which happens to a lot of theatre actors, then we (the audience) sense inauthentic behavior.

Reinking

chapter four

The Different Styles of Auditioning

You are well aware that there are various types of TV shows. Do you know that each type has a very specific set of audition rules? Auditioning for a sitcom is very different from auditioning for a crime drama. I learned this in The Room by sorting out what works for each genre, and what doesn't.

You, however, want to go into each type of show with the right style, from the first audition. You do not have time to figure this out by trial and error. Any audition for a primetime network or cable TV show is too precious to jeopardize by floundering with the material while in The Room.

Although casting directors often teach acting on the side, The Room is not the place for us to teach you about auditioning or acting. There is no time. Our job in The Room is to fill the roles in a particular film or TV show. If casting directors had all the time in the world, we could easily spend twenty minutes with each actor, directing you, teaching you how to audition better, giving you feedback, being loving and generous with our knowledge and experience. But there is never enough time in the casting process, especially in TV, where we need you to come in fully prepared, owning The Room, and we need you to be brilliant. We are not teachers in this context and you should not expect us to be.

Occasionally, you may find a casting director willing to spend lots of time with you. Some casting directors are generous with their feedback and will let you know where you stand in relation to the other actors vying for your role. But very few. Remember, we love actors. You've got something we don't have and most likely can never attain. We are voyeurs and you're our window into the soul. Some casting directors turn that love and admiration into jealously and, frankly, use their power to make you feel miserable. There are toxic casting directors and non-toxic casting directors, and it's imperative that you have the ability to deal with both types in any situation, in any context, no matter how you're feeling that day. You must learn to deal with difficult people. It's easy for you to get sucked into their energy because you need their approval so badly. Avoid this energy drain at all costs. Be sure of yourself, come in prepared, and never come in needy or desperate.

The following tips were formulated through fifteen-plus years of watching auditions run by the best casting directors in town, running countless auditions myself, and directing thousands of actors. I very often molded their auditions to help them book the job. This insider information is not available from other actors, acting coaches, or even producers/directors, unless they have served as casting directors at some point. An actor is a special type of person; acting is a mysterious talent. Most folks do not know how to handle or communicate with you. The better casting directors do.

1: Multiple-Camera Sitcoms

These shows rehearse for five days before shooting in front of a live audience with four cameras. The most famous ones are "I Love Lucy" (which originated the Multiple-Camera system), "Cheers," "Frasier," "Friends," and "Will and Grace." The multi-camera coverage simultaneously collects four different angles as the scenes play out, usually on a sound stage. It's shot in front of an audience, sitting on bleachers much like a little league baseball game, which has been "warmed up" by a comic. It's a lot of fun to take part in, both as an audience member and as an actor. In 2009, this type of show was on the decline, but it now seems to be showing a resurgence with new shows like "Whitney," "Mike and Molly," "Two Broke Girls," as well as returning hit shows such as "Big Bang Theory" and "Two and a Half Men."

A sitcom is the only type of primetime episodic TV show that rehearses the same script for four days and shoots on the fifth. The director blocks the show – giving the actors their movements and activities - much like a play, and there are run-throughs of the whole script for the writer/producers at the end of each day. After the run-throughs, the actors go home and the writer/producers go back to the writers' room and revise the script, sometimes late into the night.

Most of the other TV shows do not rehearse at all or rewrite on a daily basis. This is also the only type of TV show where the actors take off every fourth week. It's a great schedule for actors.

In The Room, sitcom material must be performed letter perfect. You cannot paraphrase. You cannot add "ahs" or "ums." You cannot invert a line. If you do so, you will destroy its rhythm and sabotage the delivery the writers painstakingly labored to achieve. Think of it as witty repartee in a Noel Coward play. You would not paraphrase Coward's lines. You would not paraphrase Shakespeare's lines. It is all about rhythm and comic timing.

If you change the syntax or the punctuation of the line, you destroy it.

The timing is quick and witty, like the dialogue in a Woody Allen comedy. You cannot take too much time within the scene. Once it slows down, you will kill the energy and the quick-witted pace. The lines need to overlap each other, like a funny conversation in real life.

As I said previously, the writer is the producer. Generally, your callback will be in front of the episode's writer, and changing his or her lines will piss them off.

The energy you bring into the audition should be bright, but not too bright. Don't try to be too funny. If you have a natural sense of humor and you stick to the words, it will be funny. Let the words do the work for you. If you try to be funny, it will seem forced and we will just roll our eyes and go on to the next person. If you don't have a natural sense of humor, then you're not going to thrive in sitcoms anyway.

I cut my teeth in the sitcom world and was witness to countless auditions in which actors would try to make their auditions unique by adding an accent or creating a larger-than-life character that was a caricature. Some actors used strange gestures in order to make the material funnier. Some wore funny glasses or a funny tie. These tactics always flopped.

A successful audition for sitcoms requires intelligence, excellent timing, precision, clarity, and a comprehensive grasp of the language. Nothing more, nothing less.

And a word of warning, given from the heart: When you're booked on a sitcom, you must bring your "A" game to the table read, rehearsals, and shoot day. You can't be too casual on the set with the rest of the cast just because the series regulars are acting like it's no big deal. They're under contract, secure in their jobs on the show, and often won't know their lines until the day of the shoot. You are a visitor in their world. You must be a perfect person and know your lines, even when they change constantly. You must not challenge the director, ask too many questions, or be too friendly with the stars. I've seen too many actors get recast, sometimes for silly reasons. They can replace you quickly and easily, and will do so if they don't like something you're doing, even if it has nothing to do with your acting.

I would get calls from the set often. In one case, the assistant director complained to me of an actor who was making personal phone calls from the set phone. In another instance, I got a call from the show runner about an actress with an overblown opinion of herself, refusing to eat with the extras, sitting on people's laps, and being a little too friendly.

I joked with this show runner by saying, "So, should I give each actor a personality test before I send them to the stage?" The answer was yes. The casting director is responsible for not only the actor's talent but for the actor's attitude and work ethic. Who besides the casting director is the producer or assistant director going to hold responsible for the actor?

You auditioned successfully and booked a job. Please be a perfect human being on the set.

2: One-Camera Comedies

One-Camera Comedies, sometimes referred to as "single-camera sitcoms," like "The Office," "Parks and Recreation," "Modern Family," are also shot in five days, but they're shot like short indie films and usually directed by the hottest indie film directors. They endure hectic shoot schedules with long days and no time for rehearsal. They are shot out-of-sequence, as all films are, and it's easy to get lost in the mayhem. You most likely will not get too many notes from the director if you get any at all. And, you can't wonder how you're doing. If you're obsessed with thoughts such as "do they like me?" you will destroy your concentration on the task at hand and fall short of being, simply, another good actor who requires no attention. The director and crew have a lot on their minds, from the script to the lighting to the camera angles; you name it, they're thinking about it. They are not thinking about you. Unless you're a problem, in which case they will either replace you or be irritated by you.

All you have to do is repeat what you did in the audition that earned the job in the first place and take whatever notes they do give you. Do not ask too many questions and don't question the notes. This is a fast and furious train ride, and they don't have time to stop for anyone, especially an actor.

The audition style for the one-camera comedy is tricky. It's not as cut-and-dried as with the sitcom. It's not witty repartee. It's just funny in an idiosyncratic way. You need to bring your own individual idiosyncratic self into the audition without trying to be funny. The comedy needs to be played with great subtlety. The mise-en-scene, after all, for most of these shows, a la "The Office" or the brilliant Christopher Guest movies (*Best in Show*) is that some unnamed camera crew has parked their cameras in either someone's workplace or home and they're capturing real people in real situations, revealing both humor and pathos. We, the audience, laugh because we recognize our own boring, stupid lives in this world.

The sides you will be asked to prepare for this type of show are short and staccato-like. They are not like scenes from a play, or even from a sitcom, where there is a normal exchange between one or more people with some momentum within the scene. There is usually no beginning, middle, or end to the scene, which might be only five lines long. The comedy in the one-camera show is in the style and the situation, not in the jokes. You will not be the set-up of a joke that the star will deliver. The language is not witty. You might have one line here and one line on the next page, with a silent bit at the end of the scene in reaction to what the star has just said or done in the situation. You can find humor in the silent reaction to what the other characters are saying. You can find humor in just a look or in the quality you bring into The Room - the non-verbals. Don't try to be a character. Again, this mockumentory style is capturing real people, not "funny" people. The humor is found in the thought processes you reveal and not so much in what you say.

I was fortunate to have worked as Manager of Casting at NBC during the pilot season that produced "The Office," a remake of a British show, yes, but with a much different flavor to it. The network test for the final casting of that show was one of the first test auditions that was not done live in The Room. All the actors were videotaped the night before, each singly revealing themselves into the camera lens as their respective characters, each with their own (brilliant) monologue. Jenna Fischer's audition tape still stands out to me, nearly eight years later, speaking directly to the camera as "Pam," revealing her secret desire to illustrate children's books but instead stuck answering phones for a paper supply company in Scranton. The note she was given by one of the producer-writers right before her audition was "don't be afraid to bore us." She didn't need to embellish or complain or role her eyes. She just needed to be in the moment, feeling what the character was feeling, which was sadness, frustration, longing, hope, despair, intelligence - all very subtle, real, and with her natural quirkiness. We, in the network test, watching the video recording, laughed at the sadness of "Pam's" life, and a new TV star was born.

(If you've been given sides for a TV comedy, either in a workshop or for an audition of a show you've never heard of, an easy way to tell whether the show is a multi-camera or one-camera is by the line spacing of the dialogue. Multi-camera comedies are double spaced, single camera are single spaced.)

Comedic Films Versus TV Comedies

The world of a comedic film is outrageous and larger-than-life. The world of a TV comedy reflects the real day-to-day world as we know it. When the leads on a sitcom go out to dinner, they go to a real restaurant with real waiters. When the leads in a comedic film go out to dinner, they usually go to a strange, hyper-real restaurant with goofy waiters.

In a comedic film, the leads are normal people in a world that is wacky. The party that Michael Cera and Jonah Hill (both funny but normal guys) attend in *Superbad* is over-the-top, out-of-control and makes any parent shudder with disgust at the alcohol and drug-induced mayhem that ensues. You would not find that same party in a TV comedy. Films are more our nightmares and dreams, while TV is more our everyday life. In a sitcom, the leads are quirky in a normal world. They are more like us in a world that is not scary or intimidating. Jim Parsons and the "Big Bang Theory" guys work as engineers in what might be closer to the real Cal Tech in Pasadena than we might think. Kaley Cuoco works in what appears to be a real Cheesecake Factory and although the brilliant Melissa Rauch as 'Bernadette' is quirky and funny as hell with her high squeaky voice, innocent large eyes and enduring smile, her character as written would not appear in, say, I Love You, Man. But would Michael Cera be at home on

85

a multi-camera sitcom? Probably not. He has made his career in one-camera comedies and comedy films. And would Jim Parsons be as huge a star if he had taken, for instance, all of Paul Rudd's roles? My guess is no.

A comedic actor needs to know his strengths in relation to which style is best suited to his sensibilities, demeanor and training. Jim Parsons has an MFA in acting from University of California, San Diego. Michael Cera took improvisation classes in Second City Toronto. Josh Radnor, who has a successful career on a hybrid multi-camera sitcom ("How I Met Your Mother") has an MFA from New York University's Graduate Acting Program at the Tisch School of the Arts. Seth Rogan, who has never appeared on a multi-camera sitcom, cut his comedy teeth doing stand-up as a teenager. He has no formal training as an actor. Seems to be an interesting pattern emerging. Since multi-camera shows are most like theatre, this makes sense.

A comedic actor who wants to work in films also has to know and be completely honest with his comfort level in relation to nudity, foul language, drug taking, and extreme sexual content. I don't think the R-rated comedies that push-the-envelope of bawdy behavior further and further with every film it feels like aren't going away any time soon.

Melissa McCarthy seems to be able to do it all. Although her first big role on TV was in an hour drama ("Gilmore Girls"), she has now been nominated (with a surprise Emmy win in 2011) for several awards for both a multi-camera TV show ("Mike and Molly") and a film (Bridesmaids) that definitely pushed the boundaries of proper behavior. She is as real and down home as one can be on "Mike and Molly" and she is also comfortable with the over-the-top antics in both comedic films and sketch comedy ("Saturday Night Live"). She goes where no man or woman in my real world would dare go and she does it with infectious abandon. She's relatable, real, natural, vulnerable, and never forces the humor. Plus, she's an "every woman" in the most comprehensive sense.

Across the board, with few exceptions, TV producers and film directors want acting that is natural – not forced or superficial. Whether it is wacky or real, keep it grounded, connected, and based in human behavior.

3: Hour Dramas

Hour dramas are crime dramas, but can also be shows that infuse a great deal of comedy. "CSI" is a traditional drama whereas "Glee" and "Desperate Housewives" are current hour dramas that are also funny and over-the-top in the action and circumstances of the show. These are often called dramedies. In the middle are shows like "Grey's Anatomy" and "The Good Wife."

Hour dramas are shot in eight days with at least two days off (usually the weekend) within a seven-day week. They do not take off weeks within the shooting season the way sitcoms do. They are shot exactly like movies, with the detail to lighting, camera angles, and the design. The days on an hour drama shoot are endless. If you're on the crew of an hour drama, you will seldom or ever see your family during the entire season. If you're the lead on an hour drama, the family back home will need to be very patient and understanding because they're going to be without you. These shows are all-consuming and, sadly, not the greatest of fun. If you get to be a series regular on this type of show you will make a lot of money. So, you likely will overlook the downside. A lot of actors who work as series regulars on hour dramas call this type of job the "golden handcuffs."

Auditioning for hour dramas is much like auditioning for dramatic films. You must get very dark, personal, and reveal all of yourself. You act without any pretense. Imagine auditioning for the role of a rape victim on "Law and Order." You cannot "act" rape victim. You must be. And, while that is an intimate, scary place to go, go there you must.

When you audition for an hour drama, don't rush the scene. Let the scene breathe. Take your time. The thoughts that emerge on your face and in your eyes (in character) are what will move us, not in what you're saying. The subtext is where the drama lies.

I also believe that if one can find some little bit of humor in a heavy scene, it makes the scene more human and convincing. It brings a semblance of real life to the heavy drama.

If you do not bring all the layers and true emotion you can, your audition will be flat.

Auditioning for the dramedies is much like auditioning for comedic films. The roles and situations, a la "Desperate Housewives," are heightened in a comedic, daffy way. Only in a show like this can murder be fun and commonplace. The roles are all a little larger-than-life, but as with the traditional TV comedies, the only acting style the writer/producers want to see is natural. If you go in there and try to be funny and over-the-top, they will turn off to you immediately. You have to let the dialogue do the work for you. You can't add on another layer of funny. Just be you, a bit of heightened energy, saying those words in that situation.

4: Sketch Comedy Shows and Webseries

"Saturday Night Live" is the Great Grandpa of the sketch comedy show and really the only show of this format on network TV. The style of performing on this type of show requires a completely different set of acting skills than the others. It is on the sketch comedy shows that you can finally be "Funny." You can be outrageous, push-the-envelope, do impressions, and use silly fake accents. You are encouraged to do so. Your improv skills have to be phenomenal. You have to be quick on your feet, incredibly creative, free, loose and willing to do anything with no semblance of self-consciousness. You have to be willing to go where no normal person can go. This abandonment is what has made Will Ferrell a star. He goes places with his acting that we, the normal Joes of the world, would only be able to do drunk.

What's odd is that sketch comedy stars don't make the greatest sitcom actors. The acting style of sketch is usually too big for the naturalistic stories told in sitcoms. Will Ferrell would not be as big a star if he had stuck to more traditional television. (Hey, he ain't complaining!) Think of your favorite SNL stars through all the years, and most if not all found incredible success in comedic films and not in sitcoms. TV stories are just too small for these comic giants.

With the infiltration of cable channels such as Comedy Central as well as the sudden boon of web-based series such as "Funny or Die" and YouTube Channels, the time for low-budget sketch videos is now. In fact these webseries are so popular, especially with the younger demographic, that large commercial clients such as Nike and Subway are producing as many online advertisements as they're traditional commercials. I've cast webseries and sketch shows for both companies in the last two years and I find them exhilarating to work on because they provide opportunities for young new talent both in front of and behind the camera. They are also simply just cute and funny.

Although it is true that often the acting is not great on these kinds of shows, especially for the smaller roles, they're fun, raw, and really just there for entertainment value and nothing more, which even for me, the theatre geek, can be pleasant in its mindlessness.

When I cast any sketch and/or comedy webseries, I look for actors with improvisation experience. In fact, I won't even call you in for an audition if you list none.

The best training venues for comedy in general are The Groundlings based in Los Angeles, Second City based in Chicago, and Upright Citizens Brigade in Los Angeles or New York. In fact, whenever I'm casting comic roles, I will go to the websites of all of these companies and scan their headshots and resumes for possible auditioners.

The obvious real beauty of web-based product is that creative young actors and writers can self-produce or "put on a show" for very little money . . . and actually get seen! A lot of folks have gotten paid work this way.

5: Soap Operas

A lot of great actors got their start on soaps: Julianne Moore, Meg Ryan, Alec Baldwin, Josh Duhamel, Amber Tamblyn, and Jennifer Finnigan to name a few. Though they do not have the cache of primetime shows, soap operas offer contract work with decent pay. And, they provide a great training ground for camera work. You work virtually every day and get to develop a character over a long span of time. If you're a young actor, extremely good-looking, and can act, you'll probably be guaranteed work (as much as one can guarantee work in this business).

Having said the above in 2009, I now have to add that soaps don't dominate the daytime airwaves like they used to. In fact, there were 19 soaps being broadcast on network TV in 1969 and 12 in 1990. Since January of 2012, only four daytime soaps remain – "General Hospital," "Days of our Lives," "The Young and the Restless," and "The Bold and the Beautiful."

My take on soaps is that the material tends to be sentimental and precious. Always try working against that when auditioning, otherwise, the writing could sound worse than it is.

6: Commercials

During my years casting episodic TV and films in Los Angeles, I never once cast a commercial. It's rare that a casting director on either coast juggles "theatrical" casting (meaning episodic TV and films) with the casting of commercials. They are usually two different worlds with different agents and agencies, clients, and processes.

From 2006-2010, I helped run a casting company in Denver, Colorado, with Sylvia Gregory ("Reinking-Gregory Casting") and we pretty much covered all of Colorado. Since there are no TV shows produced in that state and the film work was rather limited and low paying, we mainly cast commercials. We worked on regional commercials, such as for the Colorado Lottery (which were a lot of fun!) and Banner Health, and we worked on national commercials for clients such as Honda, Duracell, Nike, and Furniture Row.

There is an art to auditioning and working in commercials, and in no way can an actor book a commercial without talent and charisma and all the other elements that have been discussed in this book so far. It makes me nervous when a newbie will say off-handedly, "Oh, I'll just get work in commercials and voice-overs if all else fails." Booking acting jobs is hard no matter what the medium is you're auditioning for.

The following are what I consider the three basic jobs to be found on-camera in commercials:

Spokespeople. These jobs can range from walking around a furniture display, explaining the good deal and excellent design elements to be found in the merchandise of this particular store, or it can be the character of 'Flo' in the Progressive car insurance ads, who has now become a national icon. A good spokesperson is hard to find. You have to make rather dry material, such as the stats of a car engine, sound natural and conversational.   You have to take sentences that you would never say in real life and make them warm and accessible.   You have to be enthusiastic about the product but you can't sell. A common note a client in the audition room will give an actor is "tell, don't sell."   If you're stiff and not revealing your personality in The Room, if you trip over the words, if you can't walk and talk at the same time, you will not book this kind of work.

If you do book this kind of work, as did Stephanie Courtney who is 'Flo,' it can change your life as much as a pilot and series can, in relation to money and exposure. Stephanie has been an accomplished actress for years, in theatre, TV, film, and with The Groundlings, but now her financial life is stable, which is a gift for an actor. There is no longer a stigma to doing commercial work. Being the Mac in

Apple's "Get a Mac" campaign certainly didn't hurt Justin Long's career!

Dialogue within the commercial. This type of audition is when you're doing a "scene" - although a very short one, it is still a scene between you and one or more others. The dialogue can either be witty banter between you and your "girlfriend" related in some way to beer, or it can be a heartfelt discussion between you and your "daughter" related to what cell phone coverage to choose. You have less than thirty seconds to reveal yourself within the context of the scene. You are usually doing the scene with another actor or two, so you must also be a generous and equal scene partner, just as you would in a play. If you make it all about "you" and trying to stand out, you'll destroy the delicacy of the scene and the chemistry that absolutely needs to be created between the actors for us to be engaged in what is going on. If we think you're a "show off" we won't hire you.

A subtle humor, like those found in the one-camera comedies, is very common in these commercials. In fact, for at least three years now, the common character description and prototype we get from the client about what or who they're looking for is "Ed Helms from 'The Office'" or "Aubrey Plaza from 'Parks and Rec'." We look for actors with an easy way with comedy, who aren't working too hard at being funny. We also look for strong improv skills because it's inevitable you will be asked to "go off book" and improvise the situation with your scene partner. Usually the copy is so short that we need to get a stronger sense of you and how spontaneous and loose you can be in a pinch if the scene as written isn't working. Improv weeds out the strong from the weak, so to speak.

These auditions not only involve dialogue but, more importantly, they involve actions such as brushing your teeth while your wife talks to you or cheering at a football game while drinking a Coke. And since you're doing these activities on camera, you're confined to the space you can use. Your actions need to be focused, precise and best well thought-out before you come in The Room. Sometimes you can use actual props and sometimes you have to mime, so not only do you have to be strong at improv, you have to be good at pantomime. So who thinks booking commercials is easy?

Type-wise, clients are choosing actors who are not too studly for the men and not too gorgeous for the women. The Everyman and Everywoman, those actors with whom the consumer can best identify. I've seen clients more often than not pass on an actress because she's too pretty, presuming she will intimidate the rest of us normal folks into not buying the product. The more "normal" an actor is, the more he will work in commercials.

Non-speaking roles. These commercials where you don't speak involve you doing something while a song or voice over plays underneath. It could be a Bud commercial where a bunch of guys are having fun at a bar and checking out hot women, or it could be just you smiling, eating pie at a Marie Callender's. Your face might go by in a nanosecond but, believe me, the clients will debate over who's the best face to represent their product. They take nothing lightly and in fact are as hard to please as the producers and network executives who work in episodics.

As with episodics, clients look for actors who don't mug for the camera. They choose actors who make it look natural and easy. They hate actors who overreact reactions. Since you're not speaking at all in these types of auditions, it's all about your reactions, it's all about your thoughts reflecting on your face and in your eyes. Keep it real but also reveal yourself in everything you do.

In conclusion regarding commercial acting, beware of direction to be goofy or over-the-top. Always keep the work grounded, make it clever but not stupid, funny but not obnoxious. There is a fine line between what is endearing and what is just gross and inauthentic. That line divides getting the job from not getting it.

Oh, and don't fast forward through the commercials when you're watching TV. They are free acting classes.

Reinking

chapter five

How Do We Choose Who Gets In The Room?

Just as a writer begins with a blank page and proceeds to express his thoughts and ideas in his writing,   casting directors begin with a blank "Idea List," expressing ourselves in the actors we select to consider for each new casting job. Choosing which actors to bring in to The Room or offer a part to directly is a complicated process and requires as much sensitivity and insight as that of a poet. I have a script in front of me - could be a classic play such as *Romeo and Juliet*, an episode from a network TV show such as "Arrested Development," or a cute commercial for Honda - and I have hundreds if not thousands of actors to choose from for the roles I need to cast. Who will I choose?

I bring in actors I already have a connection with and I audition actors who are new to me, submitted by an agent, manager or through *Actors Access* (an online service run by Breakdown Services through which actors with no representation can self-submit).

The actors I already have a connection with come into my sphere from so many different resources. I watch TV shows, I see films and I sniff out cool webseries on the Internet. I take note of the actors I think are good in all these mediums and jot their name down. I lead workshops and keep the headshots of the actors who have impressed me with their natural charisma and ease. I have bins and bins of *Playbills* and other programs from plays with little stars or hearts next to the name and headshot of the actor who moved me.

I   become a "fan," in a way, of an actor, and they become part of my arsenal, a name on one of my many lists. Casting directors are master list makers and refer back to them often. I print out cast lists via IMDB (Internet Movie Database) from movies I see and highlight the actors who stood out for me. I've created and continually update lists with such titles as "Actors I Love" or "British Actors in the U.S." or "Hot Guys Under 30."   I have cast lists in hundreds of notebooks from all the projects I've ever worked on. I have kept all of my audition sessions, covered in scribbled notes, since I was first allowed the privilege of being in The Room as an intern, and I refer to these lists still. That's a heck of a lot of paper - and a ton of actors.

What's happening now, because of technology, is that casting directors can easily create and maintain an electronic database of every actor they ever cast, so they can easily find "black actors under 40" by merely typing in those words or checking off boxes and searching. I have yet to jump on this bandwagon, but I am in the minority.

So how can an actor get selected for an audition if I don't know them?   You'd think with all the hundreds if not thousands of actors I already know at my fingertips, why would I ever venture outside of my own lists?   It's a lot of extra work to meet new actors, and I'm already stressed as it is.

In truth, I'm always looking for actors I don't already know, and on most big jobs I work on, I turn to *Breakdown Services.*   As described on their website, "Breakdown Services, Ltd. is the communications network and casting system that provides the most professional means to reach talent agents as well as actors when casting a project. Breakdown Services has offices in Los Angeles, New York and Vancouver and maintains affiliate relationships with sister companies in Toronto, London and Sydney.   With clients in most regions of the USA and Provinces of Canada our reach extends throughout North America."   That's a lot of territory and a lot of actors and agents! I know when I send out a breakdown, the floodgates will open and I'll be inundated with casting ideas.

Breakdown Services was created by Gary Marsh in 1971 and has had a monopoly on getting information from the casting director to the agents and/or talent since then. It now also provides an avenue for the casting directors to receive the submissions from the agents and/or talent electronically, which makes my life so much easier. No more envelopes to retrieve and open.

There are other companies that do what Breakdown Services, such as *Now Casting* or *LA Casting* that started in the late '90s. Honestly, I like them all, but since they all draw from the same pool of actors, I'd rather just use one. Breakdown Services has the most actors, agencies, and management companies subscribers.

My process with Breakdown Services is the following:

I read the script I've been given to work on. It could be a pilot script, a single episode of a series, a commercial, a USC student film, a webseries, all of which I've worked on in the last decade.

I compose the breakdown. The information needed on this document is . . .

1) Name of Project

2) Format - is it a multi-camera sitcom? webseries? short film?

3) Network and studio attached, if for a TV show

4) Production Company name, if for a film

5) Client name, if for a commercial or new media

6) Casting Director Name (along with associates and assistants if any)

7) Director name

8) Writer name

9) Producer(s) name(s)

10) Dates of Shoot

11) Dates of Casting Session

12) Pay Rate

13) Contract - SAG-AFTRA or Non-Union.

Brief Description of the Project - ("Jeff and Ravi Fail History" is a webseries for SUBWAY that is being produced by a select team of USC (Graduate) Film School students. The initial order is for three episodes, six minutes each, but could blossom into unlimited episodes.)

Brief Description of the Talent We Are Seeking - (Seeking: Two Brilliant Young Comic actors, mid-20s, appealing, quirky, great with improv. Open to all ethnicities, could be male or female, as long as they're brilliant.)

Brief description of every role available - (RAVI (23-26). Ravi was pushed to be successful from a very young age. Having grown up with Indian parents in America, Ravi is a technological genius that would rather be reading about String Theory than interacting with other humans. He's driven, detail-oriented, and determined to make his mark on science. He creates a time traveling machine from which the hilarious antics ensue. Is written as Indian but COULD BE FEMALE, ASIAN, HISPANIC, BLACK. LEAD.)

I'll always include a statement that reads "Please No Phone Calls" and I will never, ever include my personal email within the breakdown. Inevitably, however, agents and managers will call me and email me directly. Direct submissions are annoying. I just don't have the time to go through every single one. And I will ignore submissions emailed to me from actors I don't know.

I can choose to get submissions from Los Angeles agents and managers only, Los Angeles and New York both, or all over the country. I can also choose to get Actors Access submissions. When I am brave enough to choose this option - and most of you reading this will want me to do so - I will need to brace myself for the onslaught. I will get headshots, resumes, and demo reels from everyone under the sun - actors who have just started acting, actors from out-of-town, actors who will submit school photos. I have found fresh talent this way, but this process is incredibly time-consuming and not efficient for jobs with a quick turn-around, such as a commercial or a TV episode.

Once my breakdown is complete, I take a breath and press "send." The wonderful folks in the writer's room at Breakdown Services will then format my document and "publish," sending out my requirements to all the agents, managers and actors in their system. Within ten minutes, I will start getting electronic submissions in my Breakdown

Services private-and-password-protected account. Within two hours, I could have up to 1500 of them (!), grouped by role. I am not joking.

Each submission is a thumbnail of a headshot and under each is a row of icons I can click on to bring up a resume, some additional pictures, and a demo reel. Under the icons can be found the agency or management company who submitted the actor. There also might be a simple note attached, such as "classically trained" or "member of the Groundlings."

The way I go through them is down-and-dirty, because of the sheer volume. I'll look at a page of headshots - which is usually four columns of 25 rows - scanning for type, age, look and general feel. Is it a good professional headshot? Are the eyes compelling? Am I attracted to this person? And since these headshots are no longer 8 X 10, but the size of a thumbnail, it really needs to be spectacular. (Go To Section on Headshots.)

I click on each headshot I find compelling and next look at the resume. I look at credits, of course, but also training. Does this person have a degree in theatre? Have they only taken random workshops or does their training reflect a commitment to the craft? If I'm casting a comedy, I'll take note of their improv experience and won't bring them in unless they have some.

By scanning through the headshots and resumes as quickly as I can, so I can get through all 1500, the only thing I have to guide me is my gut first impression. Yes, I might overlook some great people, but there is always enough to choose from and I've been casting long enough that I always find what I need with this process.

I narrow down my choices to a more manageable amount of actors (let's say from the 1500 to a couple hundred). I then watch as many demo reels as I have time for from this group. The way in which casting directors can now watch demo reels is a huge positive change from the olden days when we had to watch either a physical VHS tape or a DVD. Now, with the demo reels attached to the submission via a link, I'm much more likely to watch a reel than ever before. Plus, the convenience of being able to watch it from any device anywhere in the world is a godsend.

If the demo reel doesn't grab my attention immediately in a good way, I will pass on the actor. If I can't determine your essence, if you're not revealing yourself in an interesting way, I won't bring you in.

A positive upshot of new technology is that demo reels no longer have to be composed solely of scenes from TV shows that have aired or films that have played in a movie theatre. Now you can get together with some friends and create a webisode. You can write, produce, and direct a short film that showcases your talent, and you can do so relatively cheaply. It doesn't have to be "professional," but it absolutely must be compelling. If you're not proud of the work, don't put it up on YouTube. It could hurt you rather than help.

So if your headshot, resume and demo reel all combined manage to emotionally move me to think "I like this actor a lot," you move into the select group of actors I will bring in for an audition. By this time, I've narrowed down to about 20-30 actors per role.

Breakdown Services allows you to divide this select group into "1," "2s," or "3s" simply by a click. This is a much better and more efficient system than in the past when I had to physically place headshots in piles on my desk.

For my first session, I might just bring in the 1s, saving my 2s and 3s for back up if I don't find what I need in the first session. Or I might bring in 1s and 2s, saving the 3s if all else fails.

Most likely my first pre-read session will be in four-hour increments, which is about the longest any session can be before intense fatigue and boredom sets in. Two to three hours is really best but we'd like to see as many actors as possible.

Typically, we schedule one person every five minutes or two every fifteen minutes. If we're seeing actors in groups, most common with commercials, we'll schedule one group every ten. If the roles are substantial (i.e. pilots) we'll schedule in longer increments of time, but not much more. At this rate, we're only seeing twelve actors an hour if we speed through. That's 48 in four hours . . .from 1500. Ugh, the numbers!

Yes, there is a lot of competition. I'm not telling you anything you don't know. But in reality? All that competition is not brilliant. Maybe 2% of any given casting session goes really well. When you get a precious audition, be brilliant.

The difficult issue with us is that we have to wade through so many submissions. In truth, about 50% - 75% of those submissions have no business being there, but we don't really know that until we get them in The Room. It's really a numbers game, but the bottom line is, talent will always rise to the top, if you can hang in there.

It's not just about submitting your headshot and waiting for the phone to ring. It's not just about your agent (if you are lucky to have one) submitting you and you just sitting around eating bon-bons waiting for him to call you. In reality, for these kinds of roles, you have to still do as much leg work as if you didn't have an agent.

By leg work, I mean getting out there physically, so we can see you and get a strong sense of the person you are and the talent you have. In order to get auditions, we have to feel 100% that you will do well in The Room (not an easy task, auditioning). You have to be in plays and/or do stand-up and/or participate in CD workshops. You have to take classes and get referrals through those teachers and students. You have to "network," but in a good way. Not the slick I'm-here-to-answer-all-your-prayers way, but in the I'd-like-to-share-who-I-am-with- you kind of way. A kind of mutual networking where we get to know each other.

What Would You Do?

I cast a SAG webisode for *Nike* in 2010. Not only did I need to find an exceptional black comic actor, over 30, but

I needed to cast five other roles, all between 15-25 years of age, mixed ethnicity, predominately male, athletic build. These roles were one line roles. Simple enough, right? For roles such as these, I would usually go to my personal pool of actors – my "files" – and bring in actors whom I already have a relationship with. But this time, just to be on the safe side since I had never worked on a *Nike* job before, I decided to send out a breakdown. Good chance to become acquainted with some young, new talent, right? I included Actors Access in the breakdown as well.

Although I specified that I was looking for union actors only – because I had gotten a call from the signatory/production company urging me to bring in talent who were already SAG – within two hours, I received 1,800 electronic submissions. For one line roles in a webisode. Yes, it was for *Nike* and yes, Carmelo Anthony was to be a guest on the show, but it was a scale + 10% job for one day. Not for a Network TV show. Not for a studio feature starring Brad Pitt.

I was floored by the response, and to make matters even more complicated, I only had until the end of the day to set up my session and get confirmations. I needed to find five solid actors within 1,800 (and still counting as more and more submissions were coming in). I figured I'd bring in about 45 actors for the pre-read session.

What would you do in this situation? Faced with so many submissions and knowing full-well that you could not possibly look at every single headshot and resume, where would you begin?

Oh, and by this time, I'm starting to get phone calls and emails from agents and managers, even though I specifically posted not to, pitching their clients. For one line roles in which the agent will make about $47. How can I possibly get back to each and every one of them?! But whose calls and emails do I respond to? And what actors will I respond to first?? Those folks I already know. In order to cut to the chase, I reached out first to those people I have a strong relationship with.

Out of the 45 slots I had to fill, I gave about ten slots to actors who I knew and liked who did not yet have representation. Eight of those were not yet in SAG. Although I was told not to bring in non-union actors, I went ahead and did, knowing I could Taft-Hartley them if need be. I knew their work enough that I knew they would do good In The Room. None of these actors came from the submission process. I contacted them directly and invited them to attend. I had a strong relationship already with each one.

Next, and for the bulk of the session, I looked through the submissions from the agencies and agents with whom I already had a strong relationship and felt extremely confident in the actors they represent. Some of these relationships go back years and years. I think I only had to go to three agencies (out of about fifty) before I had 43 solid actors coming in. For the final two slots, I went to the Actors Access group and randomly chose based on look and resume.

So there it was, my session – completed and confirmed – by the end of the day. In the "old days," when we actually had to pick up the phone and call out appointments, I would have been stuck at the office all night, but thanks to the beautiful new technology created by Breakdown Services, it's a matter of clicking, sending and then receiving, from really anywhere. I could be eating dinner at home and receiving confirmations.

chapter six

New Trends in Casting

Type Casting

The question of "type" has become more fluid since I wrote the first edition of this book. In 2009, I wrote that "the two basic types are leading and character. You are either a leading or a character actor." I stated that if you're an ingenue, then you must be comfortable with the unspoken rules related to weight, body type, ethnicity, and beauty. If you're a leading man, you have to seem straight, be incredibly sexy yet vulnerable, and be typically handsome. TV shows and films are all about sex, after all, and every show and film must have an object of desire. It used to be that those objects of desire had to fit a certain traditional mold.

It appears to me that the cookie-cutter female roles, as exemplified in "Friends" and personified by actresses who were size zero and white, no longer dominate our TV screens. Kat Denning ("2 Broke Girls"), Melissa McCarthy ("Mike and Molly"), Maya Rudolph ("Up All Night," *Bridesmaids*), Charlyne Yi ("House," *Paper Heart*), Taraji P. Henson ("Person of Interest," *The Curious Case of Benjamin Button*), Mindy Kaling ("The Office) and Chandra Wilson ("Grey's Anatomy") all break the rules that were previously mandated. Zooey Deschanel ("The New Girl") has made it cool to be the "quirky girl." Lea Michelle ("Glee") has made it cool for a girl to be Jewish and a theatre geek. A girl after my own heart.

Although it's true that there are still female cops and forensic experts who look like they walked out of a Victoria Secret's catalogue, for the most part, we have a lot more variety of type on TV and film. I want to believe the days of NBC being unhappy with Patricia Arquette's weight on the pilot of "Medium" are over. (It didn't hurt that she went on to win an Emmy.)

As one very attractive working actress said to me, "there's always someone more beautiful and more talented than me." It's just a matter of not letting that thinking defeat your pursuit.

What is a sensitive area in this discussion, however, remains the matter of black, Hispanic, and Asian actresses, especially those just entering the marketplace. What can I advise them about keeping the faith, when there remains unspoken rules for hair and skin color related to black actresses, and, in 2012 there is yet to be a sitcom centered around an Asian family? Will the fact that there are far less roles for women of color remain true as long as writers simply aren't creating those roles?

A casting director can only do so much as far as colorblind casting in TV and film. We don't regulate the content, we only support it. But I am made happy by the sight of Danai Gurira in "The Walking Dead" and Viola Davis going wig-less to the Academy Awards. Let's hope new trends emerge from these examples.

Besides your George Clooneys or your Brad Pitts, the image of the leading actor is changing, becoming far less strict. There are a lot of successful actors now, doing all kinds of roles in all genres, who five or ten years ago would have been hard to type or easy to typecast: Jonah Hill (Moneyball), Josh Radnor ("How I Met Your Mother"), Justin Kirk ("Weeds"), Charlie Day (Horrible Bosses, "It's Always Sunny in Philadelphia"), Jim Parsons ("The Big Bang Theory), Lee Pace ("Pushing Daisies"), as well as a slew of younger actors coming up the ranks now (most from the theatre world, ironically), that if you don't know their names when you read this book, you will within the year: Steven Pasquale, Patrick Heusinger, Thomas Sadoski, John Gallagher, Jr., and Jonathan Groff.

Recent advances in camera technology have altered considerably the kinds of people we see on the small and big screens. When the predominant format went from film to video, and cameras became smaller and easier to use, a huge shift in styles happened in the way TV and film looks and feels. Feature films no longer have to look glamorous and slick, and TV shows have become more like documentaries. With the proliferation of the hand-held style of filmmaking ("shaky cam") made mainstream by mockumentary shows such as "The Office" or films like *Paranormal Activity*, the style of acting has become more naturalistic and the types of actors populating these "real" worlds are more "normal" looking. TV and films, for the most part, are now more a reflection of the world we actually live in instead of what we desire it to be.

What's also great about the popularity of films such as the Paranormal franchise and the *Final Destination* films is that they are proving you don't need stars to get audiences excited.

With the expansion of cable networks, where the subject matter for its scripted shows is far more complex than for network TV, it's never been as hip to be less-than-perfect as it is right now. The content of shows on Showtime, HBO, AMC, and the like, have become more like European films and TV shows, where the world depicted is not just populated by beautiful people. I love seeing the face of Mireille Enos ("The Killing") with no make up, and where else can the brilliance of Edie Falco ("Nurse Jackie," "The Sopranos") flourish? The bravery of Lena Dunham ("Girls") to display her naked body in sex scenes when she is clearly not in shape is astounding to me. She is demolishing all the rules of TV casting and I find that very exciting. What matters in cable shows, above type, is that the acting be superb.

The bottom line is that, more than ever, there is now an opportunity for all types of actors to find good roles. You absolutely do not have to come in The Room trying to be someone you're not. You don't have to change a thing. Just come in as yourself, quirks and all. In fact, the quirkier the better.

In keeping with this idea of authenticity in The Room, I would have to advise a black actress to audition with her natural hair. Is this a controversial stance as evidenced by the fact that Viola Davis's decision to go wig-less to the Oscars was newsworthy and bordered on a huge political statement? Perhaps so, but it might be worth considering. The Room is not about your hair, it's about your face, your eyes, and first and foremost, the emotional connection you create with us.

Please do not get discouraged by remarks like "You are too tall" (for women), or "You aren't pretty/handsome enough." Some actors have been told "It's hard to type you." But this comment didn't daunt Michael Emerson ("Lost," "Person of Interest") from pursuing his ambition to be a working actor. Even he couldn't have imagined that his years starring in plays at the Alabama Shakespeare Festival would lead him to make a very successful career playing deranged killers. I was present at his very first on-camera audition, and I can tell you, he's an actor who comes into an audition as himself, comfortable with who he is. He is self-aware, not self-conscious.

If you're confused at all about where you fit in, instead of wondering what type you are, I would suggest you start a list of actors who are taking your roles. Watch movies and television shows and start taking note of the actors who are in the roles you might be right for. Be honest with yourself; you might admire Rachel McAdams, but is she taking your roles? You might, instead, be more like an Aubrey Plaza. We need as many Aubrey Plazas as we need the Rachel McAdams.

Having said this, why can't a young attractive black actress who is well-trained and talented say that Rachel McAdams is taking her roles? The difference seems to be only about skin color. Will the day come soon when a leading ingenue role will be played by an actress of color in a mainstream film that isn't race specific? The definition of ingenue is "beautiful, gentle, sweet, virginal, and often naïve." I could not find a definition that included Caucasian.

The Well-Rounded Actor is Golden

Now, more than ever, the only way for an actor to make a living at acting is to have the agility to work in TV, film, commercials, new media, and theatre. In order to give up your day job and make your income solely on acting, you have to be good at auditioning for all media. In order to feed your soul, you have to be able to do plays. Performing in plays affords an actor the opportunity to collaborate on an artistic endeavor that is stimulating, intellectual, emotional, and physical.

As I've said before, I'm biased toward well-trained theatre actors. Although I enjoy actors like Seth Rogen and admire Jonah Hill (who by the way is amazing in The Room!), I get most excited by those actors whose background is in traditional theatre and musicals. I believe that theatre training is the best foundation for an actor. It allows a safe place for actors to learn who they are as performers. It's where an actor learns how to analyze a script and how to break down a character. It provides the actor with technique and a working knowledge of Constantin Stanislavski (The Method), Michael Chekhov, Sandy Meisner, and all the other great acting teachers of the past. Voice and movement classes are also essential to the actor's craft. The theatre offers an actor discipline and knowledge beyond acting.

So many great TV actors come from theatre; Laurie Metcalf, Christine Baranski, Lea Michelle, Matthew Morrison, Jesse Tyler Ferguson, Michael Emerson, Bryan Cranston, Josh Radnor, and to some extent Neil Patrick Harris, who started as a kid on a TV show but has since juggled his on-camera work with musical theatre (*Assassins, Company*).

One of the many joys of working on "Frasier" was that all the writer-producers on that show truly appreciated good theatre actors. David Hyde Pierce, John Mahoney, and Kelsey Grammer all come from the theatre. On the show, we stole from the New York and London stages all the time: Sir

Derek Jacobi (playing a terrible Shakespearian actor), Nathan Lane, Brian Stokes Mitchell, Carolee Carmello, Jean Smart, Harriet Sansom Harriet, to name only a few. They were all brilliant and could handle with ease the erudite and witty language of the show.

In some circles, there is a bias against theatre and theatre training. When I taught "Acting and Directing for the Camera" at University of Colorado, Boulder, where we brought together twenty filmmakers from the film studies department and twenty actors from the theatre department, I could feel the initial unspoken tension between the theatre and film students. Not with all the students but enough to make it uncomfortable. The actors didn't think the filmmakers knew how to talk to actors and the filmmakers thought the actors were "too theatrical." All too often, people get lumped into stereotyped categories, and for some odd reason, those who love and study theatre experience the worst of it.

Describing an actor as being "too theatrical" means that the actor is not authentic, and any actor, whether they do plays or have never stepped foot on a stage, can be inauthentic. I hate that the theatre stigma is bandied about so broadly and applied blindly to all theatre trained actors.

Kelsey Grammer, who is a trained theatre actor, is not subtle. In fact, some might call him "theatrical," but he has great depth, so it never seems like he is overacting. He won many Emmy® Awards for being larger-than-life. The same can be said about John Lithgow, Sean Hayes, and Glenn Close. If another actor who has no depth were to do what they do, it would be unbearable to watch.

Actors have to find their own calibration for camera work, whether they're theatre actors or not. On-camera work, especially with dramatic film and TV shows, is all about the eyes. All the energy you might put into your whole body on stage now must all be focused in your eyes. It is through the eyes that we see into you. Seeing your thoughts moves us.

A common misconception younger theatre actors have, however, confuses being more natural with doing nothing. Some tone down so much that they literally have nothing going on in their eyes and can appear robotic. Doing too much and doing too little are equally ineffective. Each actor has to find the perfect balance where he or she is natural, real, and showing the full range of human emotion reflected in the eyes. If you follow the precepts of charisma discussed earlier - being relaxed, showing vulnerability, showing your true self, being a good listener, revealing your natural sexiness, etc. - then you will find your on-camera self. You will be wonderful, we will fall in love with you, and you will book jobs.

It's shortsighted and unrealistic to come into this business with the goal of being just a movie actor. Practically speaking, it's far more difficult to get cast in a film than any other medium. Even though it seems that everyone and their mother is making a movie these days, there are less films than ever before being produced in the traditional studio system, where the actors are paid a union wage. And even in a studio film, only the stars get paid a substantial amount of money; all the other actors in the roster get paid "scale plus ten percent," scale dependent on which SAG contract is being used on the film. The contract depends on the budget of the film. Scale, which is contractually the minimum amount an actor can be paid, could be $800 a day, it could be $100 a day.

In the case of the microbudget films that are currently all the rage, the actor's salary is often "deferred." An actor won't get paid if the film never finds distribution. Most indie films never get finished let alone get distributed. For every *Take Shelter* or *Martha Marcy Mae Marlene,* there are thousands of films out there being made in every burg and every corner of the globe, that never see the light of day.

Just as an actor can't make a living just being in movies, an actor can't make a living just being a regional theatre actor.   Maybe with the exception of the Oregon Shakespeare Festival in Ashland, the days of an actor being employed full-time, all-season-long by a prestigious theatre company such as Steppenwolf in Chicago or South Coast Repertory in Southern California are long gone. I know some exceptional actors who have devoted their entire careers to the regional theatre system and are now in their 50s or older. Most feel that they have nothing to show for all their hard work. They have little or no film for posterity, and they don't have the amount of money that their successful colleagues in film and TV have at this point in their lives. They also lack the network and cable TV credits that can get them into the audition rooms. In the worst cases, theatre actors have had to either leave the business entirely or take on side jobs that are menial such as flower delivery to make ends meet. Alas, I know many brilliant actors in this category. I suppose this is the plight of any true artist living in America - living hand-to-mouth just to be able to do what you love. Perhaps that's a discussion for another book.

What this book is about, of course, is how to make a living as an actor, and the bread and butter of any working actor's life in today's marketplace are TV roles. There are more roles available in this medium than any other. Major film stars have worked in TV - Will Smith, Tom Hanks, Denzel Washington, George Clooney, Shia LaBeouf (who was on the Disney Channel's "Even Stevens"), and Ryan Gosling, who was a Mouseketeer. If there ever was a stigma against a film actor doing TV, it no longer exists.

An actor needs to be able to do it all to keep working. Allison Janney's career is a prime example of the well-rounded career I'm talking about. This award-winning actress is a theatre trained actor who has appeared on Broadway (A *View From The Bridge, Present Laughter, 9 to 5*), soap operas ("Guiding Light"), hour dramas ("West Wing"), single-camera comedies ("Mr. Sunshine"), Sundance films (*Juno*), studio films (*The Help*), and is the voice of *Kaiser Permanente* in their commercials. She's not easy to typecast and as a young actress she was told her height (6') was a detriment. She has been quoted as saying, "Years ago, one casting agent told me that the only roles I could play were lesbians and aliens."

Zoe Kazan is also living the dream of any working actor. She has starred Off-Broadway, Broadway (I had the great fortune to have seen her in *The Seagull* a few years ago where she blew me away), in huge feature films (*It's Complicated, Revolutionary Road, In the Valley of Elah*), microbudget films (*The Exploding Girl*), and TV ("Bored to Death").   She takes it one step further by also being a playwright   (*We Live Here* premiered at Manhattan Theatre Club in 2011).

Having a well-rounded acting career is the key to staying fresh, stimulated, and continuing to grow and learn as a person. Film and TV will pay the bills and get you attention, theatre will allow you to work on roles and texts that are inspiring, reminding you of why you're an actor in the first place.

Talking With . . . Sarah Drew

Sarah currently stars on "Grey's Anatomy" as Dr. April Kepner. Other TV credits include "Mad Men," "Glee," "Supernatural," "Private Practice," "Medium," and many more. Films are: Radio, American Pastime, Tug, Weiners. Theatre credits include: Vincent in Brixton (Broadway and London), Third (The Geffen Playhouse), Romeo and Juliet, Arcadia , Heartbreak House, Uncle Vanya (various).

CR: Sarah, I'm interviewing you for this book because, from the perspective of a young actor ready to graduate from a theatre training program, you have the dream career. You graduated from the University of Virginia with a degree in theatre, worked successfully as a stage actress in New York, relocated to Los Angeles, eventually landing a series regular gig on a beloved network TV show, and all before turning thirty.

SD: Yes, I miss theatre and would love to do more film, but I just happened to fall more into the TV world.

CR: How long have you been out of school?

SD: Ten years.

CR: And can you please tell me about your first few years auditioning for on-camera work after training so long in theatre? How well were you prepared for that tricky transition?

SD: Most of my training at school was in theatre, yes. I only took one on-camera class before I graduated. For me, it was more trial-by-fire when I entered the professional realm. It was a lot of learning on the set.

During my fourth year of college, I played 'Juliet' in *Romeo and Juliet* at the McCarter Theatre in Princeton, New Jersey. I was fortunate that the production got great reviews in *The New York Times* and *Variety*. How I got *that* job was a bit random. I did a musical theatre program between my second and third year of college. A casting director from Bernie Telsey Casting lead a workshop with us. It was for musical theatre and the only thing we were working on was songs. I'm a stronger actor than I am a singer, so last minute, I decided to pull out a monologue for the workshop. It was a bit unorthodox, but I just did it, without really telling anyone. Instead of doing two songs, I did a song and a monologue for this casting director. That's what started my career.

She started bringing me in for auditions my third year of college, and that's how I got *Romeo and Juliet*. It was only the third professional audition I'd ever gone in for. I did the show in the summer and during the first five weeks of my senior year. From this play, I got an agent. I actually had a lot of agents knocking on my door, because either they had seen the show or read the reviews. I got to choose among three very strong agencies, and believe me, I was well-aware how amazing it was to be in that situation.

I auditioned for a few things my fourth year of college. I would "go on tape," basically. I did get called back for a few initial auditions and I would take the train from Virginia into New York. I didn't book anything until I graduated, got married, and returned from my honeymoon (all in the same three month span!).

**My first film audition, after I got back from my
honeymoon, was for *Mona Lisa Smile*. Oh, it was terrible. I
tried to get all emotional but I was overdoing everything
because all my training had been in theatre and not in film. I
got myself to the place of crying and I looked across the table at
the casting director. She looked at me, with a slight smirk on
her face, and said "do you need a tissue?" I was mortified. I
went home and I started training myself to audition better for
film.**

**After about two months of training myself and
auditioning for film, I booked my first movie, which was *Radio*,
starring Ed Harris. That film was my very first working
experience in front of a camera.**

CR: How did you feel working on your first real set?

**SD: I was terrified. Terrified and excited. I was working with
Debra Winger and Ed Harris, who were playing my parents (!).
Cuba Gooding, Jr., and Alfre Woodard were also in the film. It
was ridiculous the company I kept doing that film. I learned the
most from Ed, who taught me that you should always give
110%, *especially* when the camera is not on you. You are part
of a team; it's not all about about you and your shining
moment. If you're not fully present and in the moment with
your scene partner(s), you're not doing your job.**

**I have taken that advice everywhere I've gone. I mean, I
was kind of doing that before. When you're on stage, you're
doing that already because you are always present. There's
never a time when you aren't "on-camera." But there were
other actors on that set who advised me to "save it for your
coverage." Ed thought that was ridiculous. He generously told
me, "I do my best work off camera."**

CR: Interesting that Ed also came from theatre.

How did you successfully transition from "being too theatrical" to
being natural on camera?

SD: What I did eventually learn is that looking to the right, for instance, is the equivalent of a full stage cross. The thing is, you're using your whole body to help tell the story when you're on stage. You're using every limb, every finger, every extremity, every thing.

On camera, you can't actually move your body around very much, otherwise you end up looking disconnected. So you end up *telling* or narrating the story only through your eyes when you are on camera. The funny thing is that in *life*, I am very big and very expressive. I talk with my hands a lot. If you're moving your hands a lot, however, your head is bobbing back and forth. If the camera's not on your hands, it doesn't capture that movement with what your body is trying to tell. It looks like a disconnected head bobbing for no reason. You have to learn how to still yourself.

CR: Did you feel like you were tied down when you were trying to still yourself?

SD: Oh yes! It felt really weird at first. Now, I feel like I've gotten the hang of it. Now I know how to do it and it's second nature to me. I know how to allow it to breathe and have it be real *in* the stillness. But it took some practice. The first couple film jobs I did, I couldn't watch. I mean, I watched but I was cringing. I thought I was the *worst* actress *ever*. Why did anybody cast me? My career is over! I asked myself, "what are you doing with your eyebrows?! Gosh, stop scringing up your face!" But I really learned by watching my work on television.

The strong TV and film directors will call you out when you're doing too much. They will say something to the effect, "the whole story is in your eyes. All you have to do is think it." A lot of times on TV you don't get directors who really direct you or really help you. The strong ones will help you to stop doing stuff and trust in the thinking.

You feel like you're not doing anything. You can't help but ask, "how can anyone be interested in watching this?!" But

because the camera is so close, the eyes really do become the windows to the soul. You think it and it shows up.

CR: So how has being on "Grey's Anatomy" changed your life, for both better and for worse?

SD: I can't think of anything for worse. Honestly, I'm constantly pinching myself every day. Even watching the episodes on TV every week is a joy. I know what's going to happen and yet I still find myself weeping. I can't believe what a great show it is week after week and that I get to be a part of it. I feel incredibly grateful. I think the writing is fantastic. We have amazing actors on our show. The stories are so thought provoking and emotionally moving. You *care* about these characters. I could not ask for a better situation. It's also wonderful being on such a huge ensemble show.

And now that I'm a mom . . .well, first of all, it's the best show to be on while you're pregnant because you wear scrubs and the producers are so supportive. Shonda [Rhimes - creator of "Grey's"] gets so excited when someone comes back from hiatus pregnant. "Yay! Another Grey's baby!"
I'm the 5th woman on the show to get pregnant and my baby (son Micah) is the 13th baby to be born while the show has been in production. You're not working constantly crazy hours. You have breaks (in the schedule). It's the best of every possible world.

CR: Can you tell me a little bit about the audition process you had to go through to get that show.

SD: Well, I didn't audition for it, actually. I did two episodes on "Private Practice," which is also Shonda's show. As a direct result of being a guest star on that show, I booked her pilot that she did a few months later (2009) - "Inside the Box." It was an amazing pilot but didn't get picked up for series, which still

really baffles me. It was a great show. After working with her on that, Shonda then wrote me the part on "Grey's."

CR: Wow, you are a lucky actress.

SD: Yeah, the thing was, she wrote what was originally a two episode part on Grey's. It was not created as a series regular role. My character was coming on the show to get fired at the end of my second episode and I knew that going into it. I thought, "awesome, love working for her, so excited." I did my two episodes and the morning after my second episode aired, the one in which I got fired, I got a call from my agent (Jonathan Howard at Innovative) saying that they were thinking about making me a series regular. They wanted to bring me back. After that great surprise, the whole process started in which over the course of the next ten episodes I would get little pay bumps and then by February I would find out if I was getting picked up as a series regular for the remainder of that season. In June, I would find out if I was actually picked up for the next season. So what started out as a nice guest star role turned into a (prolonged paid) audition. They wanted to see if I fit into the framework, the fabric of the show. They wanted to make sure they could write stories for my character. When I got that call in June that I was picked up for the next season, I was "Ahhhh!" So excited.

CR: So going back to your audition for the pilot, "Inside the Box," what was it like for you to go through the testing process?

SD: I went to the initial audition. I got a callback. I next had a work session with the producers to prepare me for the studio test. That's usually a smaller crowd of people than for the network. Network testing is intimidating and takes place in a much larger room with more people.

CR: Do you experience nerves in such a situation?

SD: I actually enjoy going into a room full of people because it feels like doing a play in a little black box theatre. At ABC, the test is actually in a theatre setting. At the studio test, it's always more warm and friendly. You've already been working with most of the folks in this room and so there's a familiarity and working relationship established. There's more conversation. It's warmer.

At the network test, it's more like a performance. You walk into the room and it's set up like a stage. It looks like a black box theatre. There are rows of seats and a stage. You are lit so you don't see the 30 people or so who are watching you.

There's no chit-chat to make you feel comfortable. You go to your mark, you sit down, you smile, the lights are shining on your face, and you starting doing your scenes. I thrive in this situation. Also, by the time you get to the network test, you've worked on the scenes so much and you've done them so many times, they are in your body, they are in your soul. You really don't have to worry about anything.

CR: And did you get to do your scenes with an actor?

SD: No. It's done with the casting director.

CR: It's funny, but it feels like in the network test, it's bringing together both your theatre experience and your on-camera knowledge.

SD: That's true. In fact, the network test is taped. You are being watched on camera, in the monitors. I wonder if they go back and watch those tapes. I wonder about this because you usually find out within an hour from when you leave the test whether you booked the job or not. They make that decision right in that room, before they go back to their respective offices. It's all about that performance in that room in that moment in time. But I'm comfortable in that situation because I've performed in front of large groups of people before. I did that in my stage career prior to working in TV.

Reinking

chapter seven

Transition From Amateur to Professional

I have lectured and held audition workshops at university theatre programs and acting schools around the country and shared my knowledge with so many fine young actors. Most feel overwhelmed at the prospect of making the transition from theatre to on-camera work. This section is dedicated to them and my desire to calm their fears.

Relocating for Work

As it stands now, New York and Los Angeles are the only cities in which one can make a living as a full-time actor. If you are a part-time actor or hobbyist, then there is no reason to move. Moving is costly in many ways and can be traumatic emotionally. If your goal is to be a full-time working actor, however, there is no question that you absolutely must relocate and there is no reason to delay the inevitable.

For those actors who are just graduating from either high school or college, the following applies:

It's easier to get an agent. If you're over twenty-five years old and don't have decent credits, as in primetime network and cable TV shows and studio films, then it's difficult to get an agent and get seen by casting directors.

You need to start your networking as early as you can during your career because it might take you years to get your bearings and get yourself together financially. Each time you relocate, you need to start over.

You are at the peak of your marketability, agility, and probably do not have a family of your own yet.

I know a lot of actors who went to Chicago right out of school to be a part of that great theatre scene. They stayed until they reached a plateau and then went out to Los Angeles Now they're in their 30s, have only theatre credits and basically have to start from scratch in a new city.

A hard truth is that credits from smaller markets don't mean anything in Los Angeles or New York, unless you're doing leads at a regional theatre. To some producers and casting directors, even those prestigious credits don't have weight.

Film credits, for that matter, from smaller markets for films that have not gotten distribution or buzz at a film festival also mean nothing in Los Angeles and New York. When an Los Angeles agent tells you you don't have enough credits, they mean primetime network and cable TV shows, network soaps, and films they've heard of. If you've just graduated from either high school or college, it's okay if your resumé has no decent credits. Otherwise, it's a problem.

If you're a talented young actor and decide to stay in a smaller market to build up credits before going to either Los Angeles or New York, you're wasting your time. Go to the larger markets and start building up those credits.

Another hard truth is that actors over 30 who need to relocate for work have a tough road ahead. Unless you're a character actor who actually becomes more marketable as you get older, the difficulty of "getting in the door" becomes exponentially harder the older you get. I'm not saying it's impossible, I'm saying the already high odds are even higher. The cost might become greater as one has to sacrifice family, relationships, and a steady job. I don't want to discourage, but an actor needs to deliberately assess all the ramifications before embarking on the upheaval that comes from "following your dreams."

Supporting Yourself

It costs a lot of money to be an actor. Truth is, it costs a lot of money to be anything in the arts. I had to take out a loan for my first year in casting. The income I received while paying my dues was at the poverty level.

Actors have a lot of expenses right from the get-go. Headshots, wardrobe, classes, casting director workshops, seminars, socializing, going to see movies and plays, therapy, working out, haircuts and grooming. You honestly have to do it all and cannot scrimp on any of it. You absolutely have to go into your auditions feeling and looking your very best.

Typical expenses are:
- Transportation Costs (car, gas, maintenance, insurance)
- Housing (rent, utilities)
- Cable (you must watch lots of TV), Netflix
- Tickets for Concerts, Theatre, and Films
- Headshots
- Video Camera
- Classes
- Coaching Sessions
- Subscriptions to Backstage, Actors Access, IMDB Pro
- Workshops
- Office Supplies
- Clothes
- Grooming
- Health Care
- Therapy
- Socializing
- Airline Travel (if you live part-time in Los Angeles and part-time in your home city)
- Good GPS System

Have a really good support system – a mate, wife, husband, partner, parent, pal – someone who can fully support you emotionally and financially. Find someone who is deeply committed to you in this endeavor and is solid as a person in their own right. If he or she is not fully committed to your success or is a jealous person, that person will not hang in there during the inevitable times when you'll be hanging out with very successful, attractive people.

Get a day job that is brainless and has flexible hours.

Try to have at least $15,000 with you when you go to Los Angeles or New York. That way, you can take care of everything you need to set up (getting an apartment, headshots, on-camera classes, etc.) and not have to worry, on top of all your living and actor issues, about finding a day job for at least three months.

If you're a young, talented, and well-trained actor, and do not have the $15,000, go anyway. Find a way. Borrow money and do not feel guilty about it. I do workshops for young actors all around the country and meet a lot of incredibly talented, charismatic actors who are at the peak of their marketability. By "marketability" I mean that, assuming they audition well, they will find work because they "fit" what television and film are after. I tell them point blank, "You have what it takes so be on the next bus out to Los Angeles or New York." Some of them come up with excuses not to go. Despite receiving a wholehearted endorsement from a casting director, they say, "But I have too many student loans to pay off first." Or, "But I have to help out my family first financially because they sacrificed to put me through school." Or, "But I need my SAG card first."

A hard truth is you have to put yourself first. You must be selfish to succeed. You must find a way to make this be okay. You have a gift and you must share it with the world. The older you get, the harder it will be for you to get in the door. You will be faced with more competition by actors with name recognition.

If you doubt your talent, if you wonder if you have what it takes to succeed, or if you're not sure you have a gift to share with the world, don't pursue acting professionally. There are too many wannabes clogging up the system.

Living Spaces

With our stagnant economy, rents in Los Angeles have not changed a lot since 2009. You can find decent two-bedroom unfurnished places for under $2000. Studio apartments are between $850 and $1100.   You can get rent as cheaply as $550 a month, but you'll be sharing a one-bedroom.   The closer you get to the ocean, the more expensive it gets, unless you want to live in Long Beach (approximately thirty miles away).

The cheaper apartments and houses are located in the San Fernando Valley ("The Valley"), over the hill to the north of Hollywood. The temperature is hotter there in the summer and it is not as convenient as living on the West Side, but it is fine as long as you live close to the hills. There are a lot of studios in the Valley (Warner Brothers, CBS/Radford, Disney are among the bigger ones), so cities like Burbank, Encino, Sherman Oaks, and Altadena are quiet places in manageable locations. I grew up in Burbank, and it was a sleepy town then and still is.

In fact, I was born in Hollywood, grew up in Burbank, and went to high school in Orange County, about sixty miles south of Los Angeles. I am very sensitive to derogatory comments made about Los Angeles. It is not a corrupt or crime-ridden place with only airheads and "beautiful" people. It is a very diverse city with very bright people living in it. It has a lot to offer in regards to culture and recreation, and the weather is ideal. Do not knock it until you have lived there.

There are a lot of great neighborhoods in Los Angeles and you can choose the area to suit your nature. If you're an urban type person, then Silver Lake or Echo Park will appeal to your sensibilities (artsy, hip, diverse), and if you prefer a small town atmosphere, then Santa Monica, with its wide streets and more casual style, will seem like paradise. You can bike everywhere and the "Blue Bus" system is efficient and very user-friendly.

As with any city, you can choose to rent an apartment, condo, or house. You should live some place that feels like home. Do not share a place with someone you hardly know, and don't stay on someone's couch or guest bedroom. Have your own place so you can lead a normal life.

Oakwood Apartments, or any other kind of corporate housing, are an option. You can move right in with only a suitcase, as everything from furniture and bedding to housewares is included. You can rent month-to-month, but they're very expensive (between $4000-$5000 per month). A lot of young actors live there with their parents or guardians, but I find the atmosphere to be more like Club Med, too much of a "scene" and less like a home. It is hard not to become sucked into the competitive atmosphere. Instead, I would suggest finding a normal apartment in a normal neighborhood, and furnish it with items you find on Craig's List.

As of this writing, there is an email list you can sign up for - The Lee List - which helps actors find temporary housing in New York and Los Angeles The cost is $10 and is run by Heather Lee, a working actress in New York. Most of the listings are shares or sublets and is a great resource to use.

Joining SAG-AFTRA

All primetime network and cable TV shows and studio films are union, whether it is under a SAG (Screen Actors' Guild) or an AFTRA (American Federation of Television & Radio Artists) contract. As of this writing, the two unions have merged to form one entity, under the umbrella of SAG-AFTRA.

The fact is, smaller markets don't have the opportunities for you to become a member of SAG-AFTRA unless you live in New Mexico, Louisiana, North Carolina or any other state where union TV shows ("Breaking Bad") or studio films (*Paul*) are shot. You could go years before getting a chance to join SAG-AFTRA in smaller markets Often, if you do become union in a smaller market, you won't be able to book the non-union jobs that are the predominant form.

Don't use the fact that you're not yet union to postpone your move to Los Angeles or New York. While it is true some agents won't sign you if you're not in the union and some casting directors won't bring you in if you're not SAG-AFTRA, some will. I have personally helped hundreds of actors book their first union jobs and I am not the only casting director who has done this.

All you really have to do to get in the actors' union(s) is get an audition for a union job, be really good at the audition (which you will be now because of the tips I've given you), and book the role.

The first job you book on a union production is "Taft-Hartlied." When a union production hires an actor who is not yet a member of the union, the casting director must fill out a Taft-Hartley form related to that actor and submit it to SAG-AFTRA. On this form, it is explained why the production hired a non-union actor over a union actor. As long as the actor in question has a headshot and a resumé that reflects some acting experience (took an acting class, performed in plays), and there were proper auditions for the role, there is usually no problem getting the actor approved by SAG-AFTRA. If the actor is not approved, then the production company pays a fine. In my dozen years of casting and filling out countless Taft-Hartley forms, only one was denied, and that was for Sue Hawk, who was the runner up on the very first "Survivor" show in the U.S. The producers of the TV show "DAG" (the short-lived David Alan Grier sitcom from 2000) wanted her to appear as a drill sergeant-type character. She had no acting experience at all on the resumé she turned in, and so SAG denied the claim. The production company had to pay a fine.

With an actor's second union job, that actor becomes an "Okay 30," which means that the actor can go 30 days following the second job without being required to join SAG-AFTRA. They can be hired for as many union jobs as they can book within that time period. When that 30-day window closes the actor becomes a "must pay" and is required to promptly join and pay the SAG-AFTRA dues.

If an actor does not join SAG-AFTRA when it becomes a requirement, the status for that actor will become "Station 12." This is the same for an actor whose dues are not current and paid up. Actors who become "Station 12" get a big red alert on their record and they will not be able to work on a union job at all until the dues are paid in full. If you're already working on a job, say, and the deadline to pay your membership dues has lapsed, then you could be pulled from the job. Don't let this happen to you! Not only will the production company be fined, but you won't be able to work and you will be in terrible standing with not only the production company but with the casting director. The casting director is the one who is reprimanded if an actor does not pay up within the deadline. And you do not want to anger the casting director.

Bottom line, if you want to move to Los Angeles or New York, don't wait to get your SAG-AFTRA card to do so.

Your First Six Months in Los Angeles or New York

I know that moving to Los Angeles or New York can seem like a gargantuan task to most folks, let alone to young actors either leaving their hometown for the first time or graduating from college with student loans to pay off. I am often asked the question, "What do I do once I get to Los Angeles?"

The thing you must never do is become complacent. Your first months pursuing acting as a professional are critical to your success and you must not get bogged down by anything other than bettering yourself as an actor.

In the book *Mastery: The Keys to Success and Long-Term Fulfillment*, George Leonard discusses how we feel about our chosen profession and how to be "successful." He posits that one needs to practice something for at least five years in order to master it. Most folks will give up if they are not making a living at something after five years. This is a shame in the world of acting. Being a successful actor requires practice and patience, just as it is with athletes, musicians, painters, filmmakers, writers, etc.

"The master of any game is the master of practice." Although acting is not a game but an art form, the same rules apply. You practice your game or your art not for any reward but because you love it, and you must practice every day. Do professional athletes work out just when they feel like it? Of course not. Do professional writers just write occasionally, like maybe once a week? No.

The old adage is that "it's not whether you win or lose, it's how you play the game." That also applies to acting. Mastery means always staying on the path, with consistency and discipline. That is the only way you will improve. You must love acting so much that you will stick with it no matter what – during the times when you're getting paid to act and during the (possibly) months and years when you're doing it for free. Maybe you're even paying to get the chance to act, what with the high cost of classes and the gas it takes to drive to those non-paying jobs.

Masters do not get impatient with the notion of "making it." They just practice what they love, day in and day out, whether they're "feeling it" or not. I contend that you will more likely make it when you completely give up the notion of making it. Besides, what is making it? Your first job on a network TV show? Your first pilot? Your first series? Your first hit series? Your first feature film role? Or do you need to see your name "above the title" in order to feel that you really made it? The vicious cycle of being successful never ends and it will never be enough if your goal is simply to "make it." Proving to your family, once and for all, that you're worthy despite the fact you chose acting over any other profession in the world is a futile goal. Actors are worthy. You are brave and we admire you for that.

Auditioning for network and cable TV shows and feature films is not the practice of acting, it's more like the final exam. If you "pass," then you will get a callback. If you practice every day and prepare with all your heart and soul, then you are more likely to get a callback and book a job. You absolutely can't book a job without putting in your time with the boring stuff, much like a musician needs to practice scales. Practicing the boring stuff gets tedious, yes, but if your only opportunity to act is prepping and doing an audition, then your head is not in the right place.

So how can actors practice every day? If not in rehearsals for a play, performing in a show, or booked on a TV show or film, what is an actor to do?

Take on-camera acting classes. Most actors coming to Los Angeles or New York right out of school have had great theatre training and minimal on-camera experience. You need to feel comfortable in front of the camera before you can feel comfortable in auditions for television and film. In most good on-camera classes you will be taped and the instructor will review the video with you. It's invaluable for you to watch yourself on tape, see what you're doing, and have the chance to improve. Listen to the advice imparted by Mark Sullivan and Sarah Drew.

Buy a video camera, tape yourself, and watch your work on a regular basis. If you can't afford an on-camera class right away, you can create your own on-camera class. With the price of technology these days, you can find a video camera in any price range or you can use your phone. There's no excuse. Tape yourself doing scenes from plays, or find yourself a new monologue to work on and tape that. Write material for yourself. Create a support group of like-minded actors, tape each other, and analyze the work.

Tape and watch yourself every day.

Sign-up for an improv class at either Upright Citizen's Brigade or The Groundlings. As I expressed several times already in this book, the need for comic actors has never been greater and the skill of improvisation has never been more valuable. Introductory classes at UCB (where Amy Poehler cut her comedy teeth, so to speak), for instance, are about $150 per month with a public performance at the conclusion of each eight-week session. You can't beat the price and the experience! Plus, if you're new to town, you'll meet other people with similar goals and creativity and perhaps form friendships for years to come. And who knows, you might be doing your scene with a future comedy writer who could hire you! As of the writing of this second edition, there are a slew of actor/writers who I saw do great work at The Groundlings back in the late '90s who are now incredibly successful writers: Ben Falcone, Larry Dorf, and for goodness sake Jim Rash ("Community" and *The Descendents*) and Nat Faxon won Oscars this year!

Before you sign up for the classes, you might want to check out their live shows at either venue. They are cheap ($5 at UCB) and incredibly entertaining.

Watch TV shows and films. I'm floored by the percentage of actors I meet who say they don't watch TV, they don't like it, and they don't know the names of any of the big actors currently working. Since most of the jobs you'll be getting are for TV shows, it's best to get over your prejudices now and start watching. With the advent of online viewing of TV shows, there are really no excuses. Watch old episodes of all formats of TV shows and analyze them. And don't fast forward through the commercials!

Watch movies in a movie theatre at least twice a month. Movies were made to be seen on the big screen. During my stint at the University of Colorado, Boulder, I made it mandatory that all my students had to see a first run film in a movie theatre. I was floored that most in the class moaned and groaned about this assignment. I cannot relate to this at all as my favorite times are sitting in a movie theatre (or live theatre), in the dark, getting sucked into the world of the film or play, being drawn in by great acting. Is this just a sign of a new "generation gap?"

Support film and please see a movie in a theatre.

The more you watch, the better you'll understand good acting and the more you'll be aware of current trends in the casting of film and TV.

Go see theatre and act in plays. Find out what are the best companies in your area. Look up audition notices through Backstage, either online or in the weekly hardcopy. Actively participate in the theatre community; yes, even if you strictly want to do film and television. Los Angeles has a great deal of theatre and some of it is very good. Contrary to popular belief, it's not all "showcase theatre." Theatre is the best way to keep yourself stimulated between paid acting jobs. A lot of my favorite theatre companies are made up of actors who migrated from strong theatre programs around the country and formed their own once they got to the city. Circle X, The Actor's Gang, Antaeus, A Noise Within, Boston Court, and The Elephant to name only a few. Go join one of these, or at the very least, go see their productions. Better yet, form a company with your colleagues from your hometown. Being an actor in Los Angeles or New York is not all about "being seen." It's about being a part of a very creative and vibrant artistic community. As in The Room, it's not all about you.

Get a good haircut and buy some new clothes. Feel good about the way you look and wear clothes that are cool, stylish and feel good on your skin. Don't try to be someone you are not, but be the best version of who you are. Yes, this advice is superficial, but it matters.

Get good headshots. The headshots you had in another city will not be good enough for the Los Angeles and New York markets. I've been to so many different markets and I know what I'm talking about. Don't embarrass yourself by submitting a photo that's not taken by a photographer who specializes in headshot photography. Spend the money and do it right away. Don't show your suboptimal headshot to anyone, let alone a casting director at a workshop or an agent you meet through a friend of a friend. You must always show yourself to be classy, smart, and marketable, and your headshot speaks volumes of what kind of actor you are.

Headshots should be in color. Your pose should be relaxed and either a bit flirtatious or deep-in-thought. They should not be too glamorous ("I'm a Sex Pot") or too severe ("I'm a Tough Cop/Criminal"). A natural sexiness always wins out and it's essential there be something going on in your eyes, because that's what good on-camera acting is all about, as I keep repeating. It's all about what's going on in your eyes and what you are thinking. If your eyes are dead, if there's nothing going on in them in the photo, we won't be drawn to your headshot.

Before you make your appointment to have headshots taken, make sure you know what "type" you are - what you want your headshot to reflect of you as a person and an actor. I would suggest doing the charisma exercises found in chapter two (*How Do You Stand Out?*). If you don't know who you are, then you won't take a good headshot. Make your list of at least 10-15 emotional qualities and try to reveal at least five of them in a single shot, just as you would in an audition. If your headshots are boring, lifeless, or trying too hard, we won't be attracted to them, just as we won't be attracted to you in The Room. (Headshots by www.amazingheadshots.com)

Make sure you choose a headshot photographer who makes you feel comfortable! If you're tense or self-conscious, that will show in your eyes and you will have wasted your money. The lens sees all, and if you're not in the right zone, your photos will reflect this.

You absolutely don't need an "I can be funny" headshot and an "I can be a serious actor" headshot. You really just need one, maybe two, really good shots, despite what advice you get from agents or photographers. The one you finally pick to truly represent who you are just needs to be superb. If you're not excited by your headshot, we won't be either. If it doesn't elicit a positive emotional reaction of some kind from us, it won't stand out. Need I remind you? It has to stand out among many hundreds of thumbnail photos.

THE BAD:
Trying too hard to be a serious actor. Not revealing his true self. Eyes are dead.

THE GOOD:

Eyes are the focus and they're alive, open, naturally sexy; they draw us in.

Joy Caldwell

THE BAD:
Joy, whom I know, is not at all the tough chick she
appears to be in this headshot.

THE GOOD:

Her eyes are vulnerable here. Wise and really "looking" at you. Lovely. The Authentic Her.

Make sure your acting resume is properly formatted. I can guarantee you, the acting resume you have right now is probably not in the right format. About 95% of the resumes I receive from actors who are just starting to make the rounds as a professional, especially those in smaller markets, are incorrect, and it accentuates the fact that they are an amateur.

Make sure that your acting resume is current, well-formatted, has no typos (you'd be surprised), and contains either your agent's or manager's contact information or, if you don't have an agent yet, your name, phone number and email address. Forget the elaborate fonts and "objectives." Keep it simple but thorough, accurate and legible.

I've included a basic SAMPLE RESUME here for you to follow:

ACTOR NAME

Hair Color:	**Contact: phone number**
Eye Color:	**Email Address**
Height:	**Reel available at: www.actorname.com**

DOB: (only if you are 18 or younger)

Television

Name of TV Show	Billing	Director

Film

Name of Film	Billing	Director

Theatre

Name of Play	Role	Theatre Name

[Commercials (only include this category if you have little or no other credits) "Conflicts on Request"]

Training

List a Degree in Theatre first, if you have one, and at which University

List a long-term training program next, if you have taken such a program

List a month-to-month class next

List one-day seminars only if you have nothing else

Don't list Casting Director Workshops

Special Skills

List everything and anything you can do. We do look at these!

REPEAT YOUR WEBSITE LOCATION HERE AGAIN –

If you're confused what your billing is on any particular role, it's clearly stated on the contract you received for that job. If it's for a TV show, for instance, the billing could be guest star, co-star, recurring, or series regular. For a film, it could be lead or supporting.

For theatre jobs, state the name of the role you played, not whether it was supporting or lead. If you played the lead in *Harvey*, put "Elwood P. Dowd" in the billing column, not "lead."

Under no circumstance should you ever lie or pad your resume. If you lie on your resume, you will get caught and it's not worth the risk and discomfort. An actor came in for me once and had on his resumé that he played 'Andrei' in *Three Sisters* at South Coast Repertory in Costa Mesa, California. He listed it as if he had played the leading role on the main stage of that prestigious regional theatre. Because I see a lot of theatre, and in fact, had worked at that theatre in my early years right out of UCLA, I knew he hadn't played 'Andrei' at South Coast Repertory on the main stage. He wasn't experienced or old enough to have played 'Andrei.' After I questioned him about it, he finally admitted that he did a scene from Three Sisters in SCR's Adult Conservatory. To make matters worse he got very defensive. This stuff infuriates me. I know how difficult it is to get cast in a lead at a regional theatre. It's disrespectful to your fellow actors and makes you look like a lying fool to misrepresent yourself on our resumé.

You can't list scenes from acting classes as real credits. You can't list extra work, even in smaller markets, even if you were a "featured extra." The credits you can list are those for which you auditioned and the role must have lines. If your lines were cut in the final edit, that's okay, you can still keep that credit, you'll just have to explain what happened if and when you're questioned about it.

If you are under eighteen, provide your date-of-birth (DOB). If you are over eighteen, don't state your age. Also, don't state your weight.

Above all, don't forget to include your email and cell phone number. We need to be able to reach you easily and quickly.

If you're sending your headshot and resume electronically, please name the file(s) you send with your name, last name first. I can't tell you how many headshots I get via email that are labeled "headshot.jpg" or "IMG_1878.jpg." I get a lot of these - most are requested - and when I download them and they're separated from the email they came attached to, I need to know who's material it is. Duh.

Register your car and obtain a California (or New York) driver's license. You are here to stay.

Contact everyone you know who knows someone who knows someone who lives in Los Angeles or New York. Tell them you have moved and would like their advice on everything from getting an agent to the best bar in Santa Monica (J.P.'s on 11th and Wilshire). There is so much help out there for you; all you need do is ask. That's how I got my first casting job. Once I decided what I wanted to do and "put it out there in the universe", I contacted my good friend Julie Haber who happened to go to college with Jeff Greenberg, one of the very top casting directors in Los Angeles His big credit prior to "Frasier" was "Cheers," my favorite sitcom ever. From that contact Jeff hired me and the rest is history. That all happened in a matter of months, once I asked for help.

Put yourself out there. What you're doing is important, valuable, and requires all your effort. But don't be annoying. Don't pester anyone. Keep it cool and real, just like your acting should be.

Mass mailings, email blasts, social media, YouTube. Sending your headshot and resume, either via regular mail or electronically to every single working casting director is a waste of time, money, and resources. If through the mail, we notice the mass mailing labels and know right away this is a blind submission (meaning, from actors we don't know). We are less likely to take this actor seriously.

Email blasts can be very annoying to casting directors. Our in-boxes are overflowing with emails from actors as it is, as I'm sure you can imagine, and there are not enough hours in a day to go through them all.

For instance, I received an email recently. This is what it said:

> Hello ~ *(this person did not use my name)*
> *I'm playing a chic, sophisticated French fashion designer on DAYS OF OUR LIVES.*
> *Monday, April 23 2012*
> *NBC @ 1p*
> *Episode 11826*
> *So set your DVR and fast forward to my two lines!*
> *You can also go to http://www.nbc.com/days-of-our-lives/ starting the next day for a few weeks.*
> *Look for "most recent episodes" on the right-hand side.*
> *If you receive a postcard today saying the episode is tomorrow the 20th, they were preempted a few times and the correct date is Monday.*
> *I hope you're well,*
> *~ (actor name)*

Honestly, I'm not going to set my DVR and fast forward to her two lines, nor will I be going to the NBC website to watch the episode. I do not know this actress.

I find this kind of email unproductive as it just adds to the guilt I already feel that I can't help all the actors out there.

I don't even think postcards work very well anymore, especially when an actor is announcing a role that has two lines. It's great when an actor books any job. I'm not belittling that. Add the credit to your resume but don't feel the need to announce it in an email or postcard to a casting director you don't know. I'm going to consider it spam and junk mail.

In the age of social media, yes, you now have the opportunity to "friend us," but if I "confirmed" all the actors who befriended me, I'd have a million friends. I can only speak for myself, but I like to keep my personal Facebook page to actors I am aware of already and who are truly friends. I do have a business Facebook page where I'll be elated by as many "likes" as I can get, but that's because I'm selling something (this book). Most casting directors who are currently casting primetime network and cable TV aren't selling anything. They are only buying and, what's more, they are very selective about who they buy (metaphorically speaking of course).

We're not interested in reading an actor's blog or following someone on Twitter (unless we know them already). We're interested in good acting. A recent article in *Backstage* discussed the merits of social media and the building of a network of support. The column was written by an actor. I looked him up, of course, as I was interested in why he was chosen by *Backstage* to write this article. Although the headshot of him was cute, I didn't think to myself, ooooohhh another actor in town! I can't wait to bring him in for an audition! My first response was, why should I care?

I proceeded to look him up on IMDB, my very first step in researching an actor I don't already know. This actor only had two film credits and both were that of "body double." I was not impressed. He had a recurring role on a Nickelodeon show, but even by the actor's own admission, that role started off as an extra and then got bumped up by the executive producer to a speaking role. He didn't actually audition for this role, which further feeds into my skepticism. As far as I could tell, from his resume, this actor has no formal training. Normally at this point I would lose interest and stop my research. In this case, however, because I wanted to prove my point, I looked up his reel on YouTube. Although the reel was well-edited, contained catchy music, and the graphics were clever, it didn't contain any moments of actual acting, let alone good acting. Did his material convince me, without a doubt, that he had the chops to audition for a network or cable TV show and that I should take a chance on him? No.

In truth, most agents and casting directors look to personal referrals for their new talent. For instance, if I, a casting director who has a strong track record, sees 'Susie' at a showcase or workshop and I think she is very talented, I will forward her material to an agent I like.

If we meet you in person and connect powerfully with you in the actual world and not in the virtual one, we'll be your fans forever. It's all about relationships, and by that I mean real relationships.

Rather than wasting your time, money, and hope on Facebook and Twitter hook ups and email blasts, concentrate your efforts on physically getting out in the world. One strong relationship will hook you up with another strong relationship, and so on.

To that end, always have a headshot and resumé on your person or in your car in the off chance that you meet a casting director or agent in a social situation and you "hit if off." I've been handed headshots and resumés in this manner many a time and if I liked the person, I was happy to receive and, in fact, have brought actors in for auditions this way.

Don't think of it as "networking," think of it as sharing who you are with like-minded people and connecting with them in a deep and meaningful way. Don't schmooze, just converse. Have a conversation with everyone you meet about what's important to you and ask others what's important to them.

Above all, avoid wrapping any topic in negative language. Negative language is a big turn-off. You want others attracted to you, not repelled.

In fact, whenever I've lead workshops, someone will inevitably make a comment about Hollywood that is couched in negative language. "I'm having trouble playing the game." "Everyone in this business is so cut-throat." "There's so much rejection." "How can I get my foot in the door when it's always slammed in my face?" These kinds of comments drive me crazy and really should be eliminated from all discourse.

First off, working in the entertainment industry is not a game, it's a profession like any other. You commit to the work and put yourself out there, as you would in finance, advertising. law, or any other line of work There's rejection in any profession, but there's always opportunity for some kind of work in this field, even if acting becomes too frustrating for you. A lot of casting directors, producers, directors, and writers are ex-actors. If you love entertainment and have a real passion for it, you'll find a way to make a living.

There are no actual doors to knock on anymore, by the way.

I recently had an email exchange with an actor who found me on the web. This is one of the emails I got from him:

"My agents have told me several times that I have LOTS of potential and that I could definitely be an Actor but sometimes I feel like they just want my money or they are being passive aggressive. I have been told that I am going to get out there A LOT for TV & Film Castings and that just has not been the case at all. This is why I think that the Chicago market is just not very good. It was just Pilot Season and I told everyone that I wanted to be submitted for as many Pilot Castings as possible and that just never happened. It just amazes me that some of these new shows and movies are getting low stars and I feel a lot has to do with the Talent. People talk a lot about how they saw this TV show or this Film and they didn't like it because the Actors and Actresses were not engaging, etc. It seems to me that Reality TV has taken over. Everyone always talks about all of these Reality TV shows like The Bachelor and The Bachelorette and Jersey Shore, etc. I think people enjoy these shows because it is something different and exciting. To keep seeing the same people over and over in TV shows & Film you always know what to expect or what Character he or she will be playing and I just feel the slate should be cleaned and new Talent should start to be cast for people to see new, fresh faces for more amusing entertainment. I attended an On-Camera Acting Workshop and the Coach made a comment which was very interesting. She said that the Talent in LA is all the same and they all have the same look and same attitude and they have all been out there for years and years. She said that LA should be looking for new, fresh faces from other markets because she knows first hand that she keeps seeing the same Talent at Auditions."

I responded back to this actor by saying that if he's already frustrated by the whole process, he should quit now. I also recommended he never send out an email like this again, especially not to a casting director. The negative feelings spewing out of this missive are destructive.

Always show yourself to be positive, hopeful, and respectful of the business.

****

I am in love with the radio station KCRW-FM http:// www.kcrw.com/ and have been since 1994. It's based in Los Angeles – Santa Monica, to be exact – but I can streamline it 24/7 from anywhere in the country and I do. It's a great resource for the best in new music – and not what's "popular" per se, but just what's really great. It's tied into NPR, so it's one-stop shopping for news, music and cultural happenings.

Recently in the Los Angeles Times there was an article by Alex Pham who interviewed Eric J. Lawrence, who is the station's music librarian. In other words, musicians from all over the world send in their material to him and he gets to decide what is good enough to get forwarded on to their world-class DJs – Chris Douridas, Anne Litt, Liza Richardson, Jason Bentley, Nic Harcourt, god I love them all. He's the casting director of the station, if you will, and I'm going to steal his tips on how to get noticed amidst all the noise.

<u>Make it personal</u>. He says to "don't waste money on fancy folders, glossy photographs and premium packaging. All of that ends up in the trash without even a backward glance. Instead, write a personal note . . . address the person by name and say why the music fits with the (station's) vibe." Replace "station" with "TV show or film" and this can apply to actors submitting via mail to agents and casting directors they don't already know. Do your research beforehand, target your submissions and make it very specific to that agency or casting office. Don't send your headshot in a see-through or windowed envelope. Keep it classy, not cheesy, and make it personal to the person you're contacting. Make sure your cover letter is short, to-the-point and that you use proper grammar and spell check. You'd be surprised.

<u>Get experienced</u>. **Don't try to get an agent or an audition for a network or cable TV show prematurely. I know most of you are chomping at the bit to get an agent the day you arrive in Los Angeles, but settle in first. Get some Los Angeles experience under your belt – at least a class or improv group. Better yet, get in a play or student film. Create a webseries with your friends. Eric says of his following to "get gigs . . .build a fan base on YouTube or Twitter. When we play a record, we're putting our stamp of approval on it and we want to make sure the artists are in a position to take it to the next level."**

✷✷✷✷✷✷✷✷✷✷✷✷✷✷✷✷✷✷✷✷✷✷✷✷

Participate in casting director workshops. Casting director workshops come in several forms and are ideal for actors who don't yet have representation. How else can you get in front of a casting director? As you just found out, blind submissions are not very effective. You can act in a play at the many great theatres found all over the area, but there is no guarantee that a casting director will be in attendance. (I also feel strongly that actors in Los Angeles should do plays not as a showcase but as a way to simply be involved in good theatre.)

At a casting director workshop or class, you're guaranteed to get in front of a casting director. We are hired by the various workshop companies and paid a stipend. We have to show up. Each workshop usually consists of one casting director, associate or assistant and twenty actors. Casting directors, associates, and assistants are always looking for actors to populate the shows and films they cast, and the casting director workshop is one of their important resources for talent.

A common question asked of me by an actor is, "should I take a workshop with anyone but the top dog casting director?" Let me answer this by clarifying the hierarchy of casting people. The Casting Director is the head honcho in the office. He or she has the most name recognition and the full weight and responsibility of the casting for any given TV show, film, commercial, and so forth. The producer or network executive hires this person. Once the casting director is hired by the production company, client, or studio, she then hires those individuals who will help her cast the project or projects.

The Casting Associate, just under the casting director, is a casting director in his or her own right. They are often assigned a particular TV show under the umbrella of the casting directors office. When I worked on "Frasier" as the casting associate under Jeff Greenberg, I was also assigned another show that I was in charge of ("Baby Bob," "Movie Stars"). Under the supervision of Jeff, I chose who was to come in for the guest star and co-star roles on any given episode and often ran the pre-read sessions and callbacks solo.

The Casting Assistant supports the casting director and the associate, much like an administrative assistant. The amount of paperwork - cast lists, session sheets, contracts - is overwhelming, as one can imagine. Sometimes, the assistant provides help within the audition room (videotaping, reading with the actors), but mostly this person works in the outer waiting area.

Casting associates are more prone to do workshops than the casting director, and going in front of the associate is just as good as going in front of the head person. The casting director and the associate usually have a symbiotic relationship, trusting each other implicitly and usually sharing the same taste in actors. Workshops with the casting director are usually a bit more costly than with the associate. Sometimes, a casting assistant will be the guest at a workshop. If the assistant is a good one, then it's only a matter of time before that person will become an associate and then a casting director. It's not a waste of time or money to participate in a workshop with the assistant: casting directors and associates often listen to the assistant they trust. But choose wisely these workshops. I'd suggest going in front of an assistant only if they're employed by one of the top casting offices.

Workshops come in many varieties. You can choose to take a one-night-only, cold reading workshop. You will be paired with another actor and given a scene that the visiting casting person provides. You and your scene partner will have fifteen to twenty minutes to prepare the scene, then all the scenes will be presented back-to-back in front of the workshop participants. It's down-and-dirty, this is true, but it's also very effective in not only getting in front of a casting person but in honing your cold reading skills. Don't fret if your partner is not as strong as you, as is often the case. Just do your best and we'll be able to access what's going on.

Some one-night workshops are set up where you do your scene one-on-one with the casting director, just as you would at a pre-read.   Some casting people use the "mock audition" technique, set up to be more competitive and most like the real world situation. This format can also be the most informative. If you get the "mock job," you know your audition techniques are on a par with actors who actualy book jobs. If you're not in the callback group, you know you still have a lot of work to do before you're ready for primetime.

The cost of one-night workshops varies anywhere from $34 (*In The Act*) to $50 (*The Actors Key*) all the way up to $75, if you choose to be seen by one of the top casting directors in TV.

You can choose to take a series of three or four classes with the same casting director or associate. The cost of these range from $200 to $250, which is substantially higher than the cold reading workshops, but you do get more face time with the casting person, allowing more opportunities to reveal yourself.   In addition, the tips and insight you will receive in this multiple class format, sometimes just by watching the other actors work and listening to the feedback that's imparted, is invaluable.

The amount of feedback you receive in either a one-night workshop or a class can vary greatly, depending on the workshop company and/or the casting person. Some casting people will give you a useful and honest critique, some will give no feedback at all. Some will share their pet peeves and the rules of The Room, some won't divulge any secrets. Some are teachers as well as casting directors, while others have never directed actors before.

There doesn't seem to be any correlation between the amount of feedback you receive and whether or not you'll get called in for an audition. The casting director who remains stone faced throughout the scenes might just be the one to love you, while the casting director who seems generous and compassionate might not think any actor in the group has what it takes to audition for a primetime TV show.

One of the workshop companies - *The Actors Key* - is one of the few where you're guaranteed feedback in the form of a written sheet the casting director must fill out before leaving the premises.

There are lots of companies in Los Angeles and New York who do casting director workshops, and I've worked for most of them. *TVI Studios, In The Act, Act Now, Reel Pros, Weist-Barron* to name only a few. I like them all and have brought in hundreds of actors I've seen at these workshops. (I'm told some of the newer workshops such as *The Bridge, The Network Studio*, and *thecastingdirector.com* are very good and reasonably priced as well.)

When deciding whether or not to do these workshops, keep in mind the following tips. First, don't take the workshops until you're really "ready for primetime." These formats will be a waste of money if you're nervous, unsure of yourself, or self-conscious. You shouldn't take workshops to learn how to audition. You should take classes for that. You must be confident in who you are and what your strengths are before going in front of a casting person. Don't embark on what could be a costly endeavor without honestly assessing your own level of competency.

Secondly, know your type and target the casting directors, associates, and assistants who work on TV shows for which you'd be the best suited. If you can't sing, don't go in for the casting director for "Glee" just because you like the show. If you don't have a natural sense of humor, don't go in for the folks who cast "The Big Bang Theory."

If you feel good about your acting and cold reading skills, and if you know who you are and what kinds of roles you'd be right for, go for the gusto. Target a particular casting office that casts many shows simultaneously and enroll in separate workshops with each person in that office - the casting director, the associate, and the assistant. This is a good practice if you can afford it. You're most likely to get called in to an audition if everyone in that office has already seen your work.

If you do attend a workshop and you do well, don't be disappointed if you aren't called in for an audition the next week or month. Any time you go in front of a casting person, you're simply planting a seed. Sometimes, the seed doesn't grow at all. Sometimes, it doesn't sprout for months. I've kept headshots and resumes for years of actors I've met at a workshop and liked. It all just depends on what we are casting at any given time. You want the seed to grow into a tree and you want it now, but that's not usually the case. Or it could be. You could do a workshop and the next day get called in for a series regular role. That's one of the exciting parts of being an actor - you never know when you'll get your break.

If you'd like to find out more about casting director workshops, go online and look up all the various companies. Their schedules and protocol are easily available for you to obtain. Choose the one you feel most comfortable with . . .or perhaps the one closest to where you live. Try different ones. The rest is up to you – and how well you can practice the Ten Secrets of Charisma in the time you're given.

Take seminars about the business. Check out *The Actor's Network* (TAN), the oldest and most reasonably priced "business information education organization for performers," which provides an endless stream of guest speakers (casting directors, producers, directors, agents) and organized support groups for actors and the like. The initial cost to join TAN is around $50 per month, but from what I hear from actors, the best money spent. Attend film screenings. Join *Film Independent*, a non-profit arts organization that champions the independent filmmaker. The panel discussions I've attended as an audience member have all been inspiring as well as informative.

Don't audition for everything listed in Actors Access or Craig's List. I think it's good to do student films made at USC or AFI (American Film Institute). It's good to do a short film that has a great script. What's not good is to do anything and everything out there that comes your way, thinking you can build up your resume with just random credits. As I keep saying, the only credits that truly mean anything are primetime network and cable TV shows and SAG-AFTRA films that get distribution. Good credits are those from soaps and shows on Nickelodeon, Disney, ABC Family, and so on. Take care in choosing projects that are non-union in Los Angeles, especially if the script is mediocre. Honestly, most "indie projects" are at best a waste of time and money and at worst demoralizing. Your focus should always be on getting cast in a TV show you've heard of, a quality pilot that is already picked up by a network, and a film with a superior script. If you can't get auditions for these kinds of projects right off the bat, don't fret. If you're talented, have a great attitude, and reveal yourself to everyone you meet, just be patient. The auditions will come. Don't spin your wheels doing crap.

Explore the city! Los Angeles and New York are cities with so much to offer that isn't related to the business. They are overflowing with museums, historical architecture and monuments, universities, and parks. Take a walking tour of a part of Los Angeles or New York that you've never heard of. In Los Angeles, go to Union Station and catch a subway (yes, there is a subway in Los Angeles!), Metrolink, or train, to anywhere north, south, and east. You'd be surprised by the diversity and beauty of the landscape all around the area. And go to the Pacific Ocean as often as you can!

Enjoy. You have taken the plunge and are pursuing the profession that you desire. Don't fret over the little things and don't complain about the traffic. In fact, I will go out on a limb now by stating that if you suffer from impatience and sweat about the small stuff, you probably shouldn't pursue professional acting.

Talking With . . . Mark J. Sullivan

Mark's TV credits include "Pan Am," "Kings" (recurred), "As The World Turns," "One Life to Live," "Guiding Light." Film: National Treasure and America's Most Wanted. Numerous theatre credits include: The Whipping Man, The Sisters Rosensweig (The Old Globe), After Ashley, Big Death Little Death (Woolly Mammoth Theatre), Shear Madness (The Kennedy Center), Cripple of Inishmaan, A Midsummer Night's Dream, Master and Margarita, King Lear, Arcadia (various regional theatres).

CR: How long have you been out of college?

MJS: A few years. I spent some of that time pursuing other endeavors besides acting in Washington, D.C. I was actually a political science major in college. I come from a politically active family and I wanted for a long time to be able to justify pursuing theatre to them. Ultimately, this was unnecessary, as my family has always been supportive of my career; the struggle to justify my pursuit of it has always been my own making.

Not that theatre always needs to be justified. Great theatre doesn't need to explain why it's vital - it just *is*, in and of itself. You have those moments, when you see great acting in a great play, where you realize the story that is being told on that stage cannot be told in any other medium. I love this art form. But I grapple with questions such as 1why do we need theatre? Why do we do theatre? Can I have as much of an impact on the world by going into acting as I can going into politics or the law? The days when it's hard to pay rent and I'm working three jobs to make ends meet, these questions gnaw away at me. All I need, however, is to go experience a play of superior

caliber and I'm reminded that what I want to do, what I've *chosen* to do, matters.

I did minor in theatre in college and was an active member in the department, doing plays not just as an actor but also as a technician. In fact, the department was so small, the students had a great deal of freedom from the faculty and they basically ran it like a theatre company, where everyone had to pitch in, doing all the jobs necessary. I had done theatre in junior and high school, so it was a natural fit for me already.

After I graduated and moved to D.C., I remained active in theatre in odd jobs, working as an understudy and back stage crew at The Studio Theatre, as well as at the Woolly Mammoth, the Shakespeare Theatre, and such, before I started working professionally as an actor.

I eventually moved to New York City to pursue acting full-time.

CR: How did you end up doing such a great role at the Old Globe in San Diego? (The Whipping Man)

MJS: The Old Globe auditions actors both in Los Angeles and New York. Many regional theatres audition out of New York.

It was a great experience, coming out to California and doing that play here. All of my family is from the east coast and, unfortunately, there *is* a stigma that's passed down about Los Angeles. That it's not as cosmopolitan as say New York, Boston, or D.C. The notion has always been that Los Angeles is good if you want to work in TV, but if you want to pursue *theatre*, you have to be in New York. I came out here and found this not to be true. I found there to be more opportunities in Los Angeles. I found the talent out here just as good as that found on the east coast.

CR: You still live most of the time in New York. Would you say the ideal life for an actor is to be bicoastal, which is what you're pursuing right now, correct?

MJS: Yes, that is the ideal scenario. I would like to be in Los Angeles more than I am right now, if for no other reason than to establish better relationships with casting directors who are on the west coast. I'm figuring out a way to balance it, but it is tricky. It's difficult for various reasons, one being that there's a lot more episodic work (guest and co-star roles) in Los Angeles and you can't be considered for those roles if you are in New York. Realistically, you can't just get on a plane to go audition for a role that auditions the next day, which is usually the case in TV. I'm finding it difficult to be considered for the series regular roles, which are cast both out of New York and Los Angeles, without decent episodic credits. I need to build up my resume with guest and co-star roles, but that's tricky doing it from New York.

I'm still trying to imagine what a well-balanced, bicoastal acting career looks like. I've been meeting more and more actors out in Los Angeles, when I do come for a job, who've been able to do just that. I've come to realize from them that the only way to have a well-balanced career is to do TV. In New York, you just don't get paid enough to live on if you're just acting in theatre. Even at the high end - even if you're doing Broadway - you're still paying out agents, managers, and taxes. You're lucky to take home $500-$600 a week. With the high cost of living in New York, that's not much. You have to find a way to supplement that income in a number of different ways - commercials, TV, voice-overs - and a lot of those jobs are happening in Los Angeles (only). So the ideal is to have a footprint in each city.

CR: And you're on your way to achieving that.

Can we talk briefly about your commercial work? You have a currently running big national commercial, right?

MJS: Yes, it's an Amazon Kindle campaign [His "Kindle Friends"Ad can easily be watched on YouTube] We shot about twelve commercials, but Amazon has only aired a few, as of this date.

Getting this great job has been a roller-coaster ride in and of itself. I went *years* going out for commercials and not booking anything. I knew going in for this Kindle campaign that the client was seeing hundreds and hundreds of actors, so I didn't get my hopes up. In fact, I almost didn't go to the audition because I was given only two hours notice and thought the odds weren't in my favor. I did go in, however, and then got hired to shoot a "demo" commercial to show the client. It wasn't even a real gig yet, but more like a pilot.

One gig can completely change your career, which is what happened to me in this case. The money I made from this job allowed me to give up my waiter job. I was finally able to solely concentrate on my acting and my auditions.

CR: Can you make enough money from this commercial to go a year without any other income coming in? A few months? How long, exactly?

MJS: Months at least. When a commercial is all said and done, you really can't count your chickens and gauge how long the money you make is going to last or how much money you will actually earn. During the month of December, there were five different spots of this campaign that ran (!). By January, there was only one. With the constant updating of technology these days, a product that we made a commercial for back in September might be outdated by March. Each cycle runs three months, so even if a commercial is currently running, they could just drop it at any time, when the cycle is over. And that particular spot might never air again. You just never really know exactly how much money you'll be making at any given time, so it's nearly impossible to keep to a budget. You always need to concentrate on how much money you currently have not how much money you are *hoping* you will earn.

CR: Do you have to keep a day job sort of intermittently?

MJS: Yes, absolutely. I work as a waiter. I get temp jobs. I tend to juggle three different odd jobs.

CR: How do you find a job that doesn't take up your whole life, so you can concentrate more on your acting?

MJS: That is one of the challenges of living in New York. How frugal can you live so that you don't have to pick up shifts at a restaurant when you have an audition the next day and risk doing poorly? What happens when you get an audition for the next morning, but you're in the middle of an eight hour shift and can't get out of it to go prepare? For the most part, there is a certain level of flexibility to restaurant work, which is why so many actors in New York gravitate towards it, but it's also a trap. It's hard work and you don't get a lot of down time.

CR: Do you think that's one of the more difficult issues a young actor has to grapple with? The financial aspect of their career?

MJS: Yes. I don't think you can or should underestimate how much time to allow yourself to prepare for your auditions. You can't overwork yourself in your day job, otherwise you're defeating the purpose of why you're pursuing acting in the first place. New York is _so_ expensive. And you can cut corners amply if you try hard enough, but still, the cost of living is a lot higher than in Virginia, say. You are working much, much harder.

When I was working in D.C., I was able to make a living working in the theatre. I was able to live off of $400-$500 a week easily. And work eight or nine months of the year. But in New York, unless you're in a play that runs on Broadway for over a year, you're signed for three or four month contracts. To make matters more complicated, every time you leave a job to go do a show and then return to that day job, there's a lag time before you can get shifts or accumulate a decent amount of hours. Off-Broadway shows don't pay enough for you to make a decent

living, so when you do one of them, you might get behind in your bill paying and have to play catch-up when the gig is over. It's a balancing act that takes time to master. I don't think I was very good at it when I first started.

CR: And as you say, the opportunities to make more money doing episodic work just aren't available in New York.

Is New York City still the best place to go if you want to do theatre?

MJS: Well, certainly, New York isn't the *only* place to go. I've worked at some great theatres around the country that aren't in New York. The most fulfilling work I've ever done has been on regional stages. But if you want to pursue other aspects of this discipline, e.g., TV, film, it's difficult if you are only being seen in one regional market.

CR: Where did you learn to be such a good Shakespearian actor since you were a political science major?

MJS: Starting out in Washington, DC was a formative experience for me. I took classical acting classes at the Studio Theatre Acting Conservatory, and worked at the Folger Shakespeare Theatre and the Shakespeare Theatre Company. Most importantly, I learned by watching and working with great actors. I learned by doing anything involved in theatre that I could - crew work, sweeping the floors, you name it, I was willing to do it. Education by total immersion.

CR: How do you keep your enthusiasm going in the dark, frustrating times? And I have to say, that you are such a brilliant actor. I hope and pray you never ever stop acting. You're an American male who can do Shakespeare and Kindle commercials. We need more of you!

MJS: I feel privileged every day that I can even *pursue* this art form. When you're in a show or working on a set, there's nothing else like it. Once you have a taste of that, it's hard to imagine any other jobs or professions. Those few times when I have questioned what I'm doing and wonder if it's all worth the sacrifices, there's always just enough of a carrot that comes my way that keeps me hanging in there.

CR: What issues do you have in relation to The Room?

MJS: It's not so much competition with other people but more with yourself. Did I prepare well enough? Or did I prepare *too much* to the point where I stressed myself so much that I wasn't relaxed or spontaneous enough? If I don't enjoy the preparation enough, the camera picks up everything and it'll show in my eyes. I always need to ask myself after every audition, did I check my shit at the door?

Sometimes I just need to refocus on the basics of the scene. What's going on in the script and what's going on within the scene? I finally have to let go of the *performance* of it. The auditions I blow are those in which I'm thinking about how the audition is going when I'm *in* the audition. Or I'll get flustered if I mess up a word or a line and it'll take me out of the scene. I have to just go-with-the-flow of it and be present in that moment.

chapter eight

The Young Actor

What do you do if your child says? "Mom, Dad . . . I want to be a professional actor."

It's best not to respond with:

- "Are you insane?"
- "Don't you know how hard it is?"
- "But there's so much rejection!"
- "Do you think you have what it takes?"
- "But there are so many out-of-work actors already!"

. . . and on and on, in any number of negative ways. Do your research before you respond to your child's plea. Simply ask your son or daughter "Why?"

If it's because they love acting and love watching good actors on film, TV, and stage - great. If film, TV, and theatre enriches their lives - excellent. If they read literature, plays, and can't wait to audition for the next play in school - perfect. Proceed.

If your child wants to be an actor because they want to be a celebrity, put the kibosh on their pursuits immediately. Wanting to be rich and famous should never be a reason to go into acting. Acting is an art form, not a way to make money. You can make money, yes, and some actors make lots and lots of money, walk down the red carpet, and have people fawn all over them, but this can never be the reason to become an actor. Agents, casting directors, producers and the like gravitate toward the pure-of-heart not those seeking fame and fortune.

If your child wants to be an actor so he or she will feel loved and whole, get them in therapy and steer them away from the acting profession.

When a son or daughter wants to pursue acting for all the right reasons, here are a few more questions to ponder:

Are they doing plays in school?

Do they want to take acting classes?

If they're taking acting classes, are they doing the preparation needed to do a good job on the scene work?

Do they seem excited when you pick them up from those classes?

Are they improving or just staying at a beginner level?

Doing plays is the best way for young actors to practice and improve on their talent. You should allow them to be in plays, and if they're very good, they should be auditioning for plays in community theatres where adults perform alongside the young actors.

If your child is very serious about this, you should try to enroll him or her in an adult acting class, or at least a mixture of children/teens and adults. Don't waste your time and money on classes unless they truly seem happy and dedicated to learning the craft. Sometimes, especially with children between seven to eleven years of age, the acting classes do not include scene work. Classes in this age group are more of a creative drama or improv class. Improv is very good, mind you, but a youngster who wants to really be an actor needs to work with scenes (text) as soon as they can read. If they're not comfortable with the rigors of scene work (studying the script, memorizing lines, dissecting the character, etc.), then they will not do well as a professional actor.

If you're lucky enough to have a child who is gifted in the performing arts, then you should rejoice in that, as it is indeed a gift from God. While you're rejoicing, you should simultaneously investigate thoroughly what it means – the nuts and bolts of being a working young actor. Don't discourage them. Talented young actors are a stubborn bunch and won't be swayed by a parent's negative advice.

Recently, I came in contact with a very talented young actress--a great student who also played soccer and excelled at the piano. Her parents were born in China and uncomfortable with her very determined desire to pursue acting professionally. Once they got over the shock, however, and realized that nothing they said would change her mind, they came to me with the honest desire to learn about the entertainment business. I found it incredibly moving when the mother of this young actress looked me in the eye and said, "My daughter wants to be an actress and I don't know anything about acting or the business. I am scared, but my daughter really wants to do this. What should I do?"

This section is dedicated to her and parents like her.

Truth be told, there are many advantages to being a young actor pursuing the acting profession.

It's easier for a child to get an agent than it is for someone over the age of twenty-five.

There is a large need for very strong young actors, especially boys.

A young actor without decent acting credits is more likely to get an audition for a primetime network or cable TV show or studio film than an adult with a comparable amount.

If your child is someone who people are naturally drawn to, great. If he or she is constantly getting compliments from people you don't know very well, take that seriously and don't be embarrassed by the attention (unless it gets creepy, of course). The attention is telling you your child has that rare and precious "it" factor. If on top of the charisma and appeal, your child is extremely disciplined, focused, well-mannered, talented, and blessed with a positive attitude, I would advise you to take the plunge if you can handle it financially.

If, on the other hand, you have a talented child who is moody, nervous, takes any kind of criticism too personally and deeply, or is angry at the world, proceed cautiously if at all. The child who succeeds is light-hearted and lets things roll easily off his back. As I said previously, acting should not be the therapy. Therapy should be the therapy.

Tips for the Parent of a Child Star

Keep your child as well-rounded and balanced as possible. Make sure he/she has lots of good hobbies that aren't related to acting and the business. Don't make it all about the business and certainly don't make it all about the child.

Do your own homework. Have an interest in what films and TV shows your child likes. Know who their favorite actors are and why. Take them to see movies in a theatre and take them to live theatre as often as you can. It is a very interesting and stimulating business, and, above all else, filmmaking, theatre, and acting are art forms. Explore and respect them all.

Work on the scripts with them. Ask them questions about the character they're preparing. Run lines with them. Talk to them about the storyline and explore the script's themes. Do the intellectual work with them.

Don't be a toxic parent. If you, the parent, are too competitive, too envious of the actors who book the jobs, and too emotionally and financially dependent on your child's success, be honest with yourself and remove yourself from the situation. If that means your child has to wait until age eighteen and do it without you, so be it. Don't enter a potentially toxic environment if you, yourself, are toxic.

You can find normalcy in the Biz. Support systems are available within your own family unit and your network of good, close friends. You also can rely on your agent and/or manager to give you advice. They have seen it all. I think a child working in the entertainment industry is not any worse off than a child who goes to a public junior high or high school. There are treacherous waters in both situations. How a child will navigate through them is usually a matter of their upbringing, DNA and the grace of God.

The Logistics of Pursuing The Dream

The truth about "Pursuing the Dream" for your talented child is complicated. The whole process - finding the proper training for your child, relocating, getting a good agent, etc. - can be wrought with many set-backs and difficulties. I've seen it from all angles. I've been jn The Room with hundreds of young actors who have come to Los Angeles with one or both parents, from cities, large and small, to audition during pilot season. I've seen whole families relocate full-time; some families thrive and some go bankrupt. I've also worked in a smaller market, specifically Denver (but they're all the same); it's difficult for talented young actors to get auditions and book jobs for primetime and cable TV shows and films while living in a city other than Los Angeles. It's difficult but not impossible. Anna Sophia Robb accomplished this. It can't be accomplished, however, without an agent or manager who is based in Los Angeles.

A solid way to get an agent in Los Angeles is to find someone with strong ties to that market that will provide your child an entrée. This requires a bit of networking, but a talented child who is out in the world doing plays, performing, taking acting classes and doing workshops, will eventually be seen by someone who can help them navigate the Los Angeles market. A good place to start is with the local agents in your hometown, who might know someone who knows someone who can provide an entrée for your child. Local agents are continually searching for new talent.

Be wary of overpriced programs such as IMTA (International Modeling and Talent Association), John Robert Powers, and ProScout. They promise your child will get in front of the "top industry folks in Los Angeles" and often this is true. These programs cost a lot of money, however, and they will take on any young actor whose family can afford the entry fees, regardless of talent. The atmosphere is hardly ever about good acting; it's all about "being seen" and "becoming a star!"

The best showcases have an audition process that allows only the most talented and marketable young actors to take part.

When your child does get representation in Los Angeles, most of those agents will not advise you to move out to Los Angeles permanently. They do not want to be responsible for uprooting a family. That is a decision to make within your family. You should choose to move to Los Angeles. if and only if your child gets positive feedback from an agent you trust.

Meanwhile, your child can audition for lead roles in Los Angeles, New York, New Mexico, Louisiana, North Carolina, and Canada digitally. (See Previous Section on GOING ON TAPE.) The local agent can put the young actor on tape and forward the video electronically to the Los Angeles agent or to the casting director directly. This is a very common practice, and not as inconvenient as it was just three years ago.

A really strong agent and/or manager can always get the casting director to watch a taped audition. Usually, it will be under one of the following circumstances:

They have requested that actor go on tape.

They are having trouble casting the role and so they open auditions to actors outside Los Angeles

The tape comes from New York or Chicago.

The tape comes from an agent/manager they trust implicitly.

Your child will usually go on tape for series regulars or large roles in films only.

Co-star and guest star roles on TV shows are never cast from a tape. There just is not enough time or money in the budget to hire from out-of-town. Living out-of-town is not conducive to building a resumé that includes co-star and guest star roles on primetime and cable TV shows, Disney, Nickelodeon, and ABC Family.

Flying out for these types of roles is an option. For child roles, the casting director will pre-read a lot of young actors before narrowing down the pool to the few who will be taken to the callback.   But it's an expensive option. (It helps if someone in the family works for an airline or racks up frequent flyer miles on business.)

A popular scenario is to live at least part-time in Los Angeles. Most families split up, with one parent going with the child, leaving the other parent and siblings at the home base. You can do this if one parent makes a decent living and the parent who goes to Los Angeles with the child can work from home.

The bottom line is that you and your family have to look at it as a long-term investment. It should become a family endeavor, not solely about the young actor. In this world of cell phones, web cams, and instant messaging, it is so easy to keep in touch with family members who are in another city or state.

Financial sacrifices will have to be made, surely, and should be accomplished without resentment, otherwise there will be far too much pressure on the child actor to "perform" and succeed. They will get work when they get work. This requires patience, money, and time.

The household in Los Angeles will most likely be based in a modest apartment, at least at the onset. The child actor and parent accompanying have to feel comfortable with this situation otherwise homesickness will set in and threat to destroy the equilibrium so necessary to succeed.

The best time frame to be in Los Angeles is for the entire TV season, which is late July through the end of April.

Some families choose to go out to Los Angeles for a month at a time. This is better than not going out at all but not the most effective game plan. An actor cannot get any momentum this way. If your child is lucky enough to get in the groove and start meeting casting directors, auditioning, and being part of the system, you don't want to have to turn around and go home right when thing's are cooking. This process is very truncated and not conducive to promoting the best in a young actor.

Once in Los Angeles, don't make everything about "making it." Don't obsess over how many auditions your child gets in a month and how much money it costs to support them. When you're in the audition waiting room with your child, don't talk to the other parents about what your child has done, what auditions he or she has gone on, how wonderful the child is. Don't make your interaction with the other parents competitive in any way. You may be tempted because some other parents will, but this behavior is selfish and annoying, so stay above it all.

Do not watch TV shows envying the actors in them. Just enjoy and be entertained. Have discussions about what is good acting and what qualities the better actors have. Go see good theatre in Los Angeles (yes, there is plenty!) and talk about the plays in depth. Make this whole endeavor enhance all of your lives.

Auditions for primetime network and cable TV shows and SAG-AFTRA films are precious gifts. Make sure your child is prepared and in a good mental zone when those opportunities come along. Hire a coach to make sure the first auditions are dynamite. The cost of hiring a coach is between $60 and $150 an hour. They might not get a second chance in some of these casting offices, and once your child's representative gets negative feedback on auditions, they will most likely stop sending them out. What the actor does in The Room reflects directly on the agent and they do not want to look bad. Their whole livelihood is based on the kind of talent they represent.

The same thing can be said for casting directors. Our reputations are based on the actors we bring in to the auditions for the director and/or producer. We have to feel strongly about each actor or we look foolish. Our egos are large and we do not want to be criticized for having terrible taste in actors.

Your child should always be in some sort of class, whether it be acting, singing or dancing.

You have two choices as the parent of a talented young actor. You can either do whatever it takes to help your child get work as an actor, or wait until the child is eighteen, leaving the decision and financial burden to him or her.

Think of your very talented young actor as if he or she were a premiere athlete. What would you do if your child were a world-class gymnast, swimmer, or figure skater? You would relocate to where the best coaches and facilities are. The same goes for a talented young actor. The odds of getting on a TV series are probably better then winning a gold medal, after all. So you need to go to where the jobs, coaches, and facilities are.

Meeting With Agents and Managers With Your Child

Once you're lucky enough to get a meeting with an agent in Los Angeles or New York, make sure that your child is ready. If he or she meets an agent prematurely, it will just frustrate everyone involved: the child, the agent, and the generous person who provided the entrée.

How do you know if your child is ready? The child must be a good actor, outgoing and poised when talking to strangers, extremely appealing and/or attractive, not self-conscious, focused, and able to take direction. He or she must have a positive attitude and a zest for life.

Save yourself a lot of time and money; be completely and brutally honest in your assessment of your child's attributes.

When you finally do get to meet with an agent . . . Congratulations! That is no small accomplishment. Make sure you and your child are on the same page when it comes to an acting career. It is extremely uncomfortable for an industry professional to be in a meeting with a parent and child who are at odds.

As the parent, do not dominate the meeting. Allow your child to answer questions, such as "What kind of movies do you like?" "What actors do you admire?" "What kind of career do you want?" "What do you like to do for fun?" Do not answer for your child, and do not correct your child when they answer in a way that you didn't expect.

Do not goad your child if he or she is not answering the questions fast enough. Remember, the agent is interviewing both of you. If there is friction between you and your child, it will kill the interview.

Don't make excuses for your child, such as, "he's having a bad day," "she knew the material in the car," "he isn't normally this shy." That is just embarrassing. If you feel compelled to offer any of these excuses, then your child was not ready to meet with the agent and apologizing does not improve what has turned into an unfortunate circumstance. It is like an actor who makes excuses for a bad audition. It never, ever makes the situation better, only worse. Bluntly put, there is no room for a bad day or anything less than a stellar meeting. An agent has to feel secure that you and your child can be sent on an audition and do brilliantly.

Agents look for a parent who is informed, humble, and balanced. They look for someone who is patient and listens to direction. Do not think you know more than agents. They are going to avoid the stereotypical overbearing stage mothers like Mama Rose.

Sometimes the agent will ask for your child to cold read either commercial copy or a scene from a TV show or film that is currently casting. A cold read means that the actor is only given fifteen to twenty minutes (sometimes less) to prepare the scene. This is not an easy task. Even accomplished actors have trouble doing this.

Since cold reading is down-and-dirty auditioning with no time to really analyze and connect with the character, let alone memorize the lines, the best thing young actors can do is be themselves in that situation, not stumble over the lines, and try to make eye contact during the reading. The actor can refer to the lines on the page but if they do not make eye contact with the reader, the agent won't be interested in repping the child. If they're worried about doing well and not able to reveal themselves, it will not be a good cold read. If they can be relaxed, natural, and do the scene as if they're having a conversation with the agent using the dialogue in the scene, it will go well.

Your child will get representation if and only if the agent or manager is very excited about the young actor.

Education Options For The Young Actor
In Los Angeles

Largely for the flexibility it allows, home schooling is becoming the best option for most families with a child interested in pursuing acting. If your child is in acting classes (as he or she should be) and active with hobbies, the lack of social interaction usually associated with home schooling won't be an issue.

Many schools now offer online options for students who must, for whatever reason, "take a leave" from their current school. A young actor whose hometown is Des Moines, for instance, can arrange with their school to continue classwork remotely in their part-time Los Angeles apartment.

Both of these options require a great deal of discipline from both the child and the parent. If the young actor is fortunate enough to be getting a lot of auditions, it's a tricky juggling act of time-management between preparing the scenes and keeping up with schoolwork.

You can, of course, enroll your child in the many public and private school options available to you in Los Angeles or New York. The question of public or private is dependent on your financial situation, which neighborhood you end up living in, and what option will make you and your family the most comfortable. I don't believe that big city schools are any worse or better than small town schools. Just as other misconceptions about Los Angeles and New York permeate, the school system needs to be looked at with an open and unbiased mind.

Once your child becomes a working actor, the schooling issue will become a moot point. In TV and film there is always a teacher on set when minors are working. Young actors are required to have a certain amount of school hours.

Being an actor is an education in itself. Some folks think acting is easy: say a few lines in front of a camera and rake in the dough. This is untrue. Being an actor teaches one about discipline, patience, humility, and tenacity.

The research that must be done on the projects and roles in TV, film, and theatre can teach so much about history, science, math, psychology, art, and politics.

Take the plunge, if all systems are a go, and enjoy the process. My motivation for wanting to share my perspective with you on these matters is that I have seen a lot – good and bad – and am not biased either way about young actors living full-time in Los Angeles. I never had to market a young actor or talk a casting director into seeing one of my clients. I was simply a participant in The Room. I was in on the first – or one of the first – auditions of Dakota Fanning (brilliant in the room at age six), Ashley Tisdale, Jessica Alba, Eva Mendez, Michael Angarano, Daveigh Chase, Erika Christiansen, Taylor Momsen, Chad Michael Murray, Wade Robson, Shawn Pyfrom, Andrea Bowen, and countless others. Most of these I was fortunate to hire. All of these young actors had "it." I am grateful that they all chose to become actors and that they were lucky enough to have families who could support them financially and emotionally in this endeavor.

Technology has made it easier for families to be spilt up, as discussed previously. Also, more and more young actors are getting cast from tape, so perhaps the need for families to be split up to begin with has lessened. I still feel that the best auditions are those in The Room, but perhaps this is rapidly becoming an old-fashioned notion.

Whatever route you choose for your family, enjoy the process. When it stops being positive and the literal and emotional costs far outweigh the benefits, it's time to pull the plug. Nothing is worth destroying you or your family in the process of pursuing a dream.

Talking With . . . Madeline Zima

Madeline is perhaps best known for her role in the long-running hit sitcom, "The Nanny." She starred in Showtime's critically acclaimed series, "Californication," and she appeared in "Gilded Lily's," the Shonda Rhimes pilot. Other television credits include: "Heroes," the CBS mini-series "Lucy," "Grey's Anatomy," "Ghost Whisperer," and "3LBS." Film credits include: The Hand that Rocks the Cradle, My Own Love Song, Happy Together, the short film Streak directed by Demi Moore, Cinderella Story opposite Hillary Duff, and the TV films The Sandy Bottom Orchestra, Lethal Vows, The Secret Path, and most recently, Breaking the Girl and Crazy Eyes.

CR: You are a very busy actress. How many pilots would you say you've booked in your relatively short life (early 20s)?

MZ: I've booked three total. In fact, I just got one. I'm very excited. For me to get a pilot already this early in pilot season, I feel like I've hit the gold mine.

This pilot season, I went in for about ten and booked one.

Last pilot season, I only went in for four pilots because most of the roles were straight offers to bigger names in my category.

CR: Can you please talk a bit on the process of testing for pilots?

MZ: Well, this last time around - the freshest in my mind - was the most unusual process. ABC was testing a different way this year from all the other networks. It was set up to make the whole process of testing at lot less like a pressure cooker and

more like a producers callback session. At the test, it was myself, the director and a couple producers. We did a work session first, I was directed a little bit, and then the final product was put on tape. This digital audition was sent to the network executives right away. With this process, the network gets to see the best acting from the actor and the producers get to redirect without pressure from the executives.

My previous testing experiences were pretty brutal. For "Californication," I had to go through what felt like a hundred auditions for that. Because I've done so much work, I don't have to pre-read. But even so, for this show I had a producers session, then a callback from that, then a work session with David Duchovny (which was taped), and then I tested at the network. At the network, my audition went very badly. So badly, I didn't want to leave the room. I asked if I could do it again, which I know is not the right protocol at all especially when you're in there with the suits. But I was tenacious. I thought to myself, if I don't speak up now, I've lost my last opportunity. Luckily they had the tape from the session I had with David, so the producers showed that. Luckily, that video is what ultimately swayed them to give me the role. I was fortunate that the producers were behind me all the way and thought I was the only actress for the role.

CR: That is such a good story, because part of the update to this book is speaking to the fact that technology has altered the way casting is done. Before, if you blew the audition in the room, especially at the network level, they didn't have any tape to go back and look at. If you messed up or weren't in your zone, you were done. End of test session. No job for you.

MZ: Yes! Also, nowadays, there are so many resources and reels of an actor online, such as on YouTube, to show what you can do. I actually need to go in and update my reels online because I'm not sure people are in tune with my most recent work. This should always be updated.

I don't even remember what it was like when I tested for "The Nanny." I was so young (6 years old). The only audition I clearly remember was for the callback with Fran (Drescher), and I remember that because I thought at the time that her voice was crazy. I was only six! I didn't even realize at the time who she was or that I was auditioning for *her* show! I immediately ruled her out as anyone important.

By the time the show was picked up, I was seven. I had already done so much work, though.

CR: Did you express a desire to act from a young age?

MZ: Well, I started working when I was an infant, so I really had no choice in the matter. My mother thought I was a cute baby and so she took me on an audition (for a *Gerber* baby), and I booked that very first one. I'm sure if I hadn't booked that first one, my mom probably wouldn't have gone to all the trouble of driving from Pennsylvania to New York to take me on a whole bunch of auditions if nothing was happening. But for that first audition, I was chosen out of 1000 babies. My mom took this as a good sign.
I would get a lot of work in print and commercial. I owe my career to my mom, of course, who had to run around New York City with a stroller and three kids, to all the auditions and then the shoots.

CR: Did you enjoy it right off the bat?

MZ: When you're a kid, you're a completely open vessel. There aren't any roadblocks. As a child actor, I could emotionally connect very easily. Even if I was playing a role in which my character's mother has died, I could understand that I was *playing* that my mother had died. I knew full well my actual mother was standing right there, over to the side. It was so easy for me, as a child actor, to get to the emotional places I needed to get to within the scenes. I never saw it as a challenge.

As an adult, it feels like we're always trying to get back to that place of openness and *playing*. In the imagination. Growing up hardens you a bit. Experiences make you more guarded. But I like to go back and remember how easy it was to pretend and be in-the-moment as a child.

Between the ages of 13 (when the Nanny ended) and 16, I went through an awkward stage, but I still worked. I did test for "The Gilmore Girls" and came close. The reason I didn't get it was that I was too young (14). I not only wasn't emancipated and the writers were going to introduce sexual story lines fairly early on. They needed an actress closer to eighteen.

I think if I would have been cast as 'Rory,' I would have burned out on acting.

Being the lead on a show, if you aren't ready for it, will burn you out. You need to be able to take care of yourself. You have to know what you can and cannot do. You have to know how much energy you need in a day to get everything accomplished. You have to have time allotment skills. For me, I have to have a whole system down and literally parcel out time for yoga, showering, meditation, and the like, in order to have the proper energy to handle being on set for fourteen hours and have your lines ready.

It can be a disaster to take on a job and not have the proper energy for it. I won't even go in for an audition anymore if I don't have the proper time to prepare. I have to feel like I can go in and do a good job. I'm at the point in my career where if I have a bad audition, people talk, and it can get around that I've lost it. They won't see you for awhile if you lay an egg.

CR: So what advice would you give young actors just entering the business at this time?

MZ: You have to be very hungry. And it's a cliche, I know, but if you have any other interests, you should pursue that and not acting. The world needs more doctors and scientists. Unless the passion of storytelling rules and rocks your world, don't get into it. You have to be willing to devote your whole life to it.

If all you want is fame, then it will be illusive. In fact, *everything* about the creative spirit is illusive. I myself have been caught up in the illusion of it. I was at the *Golden Globes* in 2009 and I was so excited when Micky Rourke went up to the podium and get his award for *The Wrestler*. But as soon as he got up on that stage, the big red light starting flashing. Time's Up, Time's Up! So even during the penultimate moment of success, it's still illusive because they are trying to kick your ass off. You have to love it so much that despite all the deterrents, which will come up, you can still remain enthusiastic and passionate *for the right reasons.*

The right reasons are beautiful. The right reasons are connecting to other human beings. Making them feel like they are not alone. Making them *feel* things, which makes them more introspective and encourages growth as human beings. This is the healthiest form of escape.

Our minds are wired for storytelling. It's been our tradition for thousands and thousands of years. It's how religions were started. We *need* storytelling as part of our evolution and growth. If you can align yourself with a higher intention, this career and industry can really be a beautiful service to humanity.

CR: Anything else you'd like to add?

MZ: You're always going to get a job when you're busy doing something else. Always make sure your life is as full of other things as possible. You won't be able to give anything to your craft if you're living a half life. And just sitting around waiting for an audition is no life at all. Keep educating yourself. Go out and ride horses! Dance! Play music!

You won't get work without a life.

chapter nine

Pilot Season

There is a plethora of information about pilot season to be found on the Internet, with more detailed information than I want to include in this book. In fact, I bet that even steel mill workers in Pittsburgh know what a pilot TV show is and at what time of year they cast. But the following is a brief overview, from my perspective.

"Pilot Season" is the time of year when all the networks produce a prototype for all the new series they have in development. The prototype is called a "pilot."

The development phase of any new TV series is as follows:

In the fall of a given year, a writer/producer with an established track record for series work pitches a new idea to a network and/or studio.

The network/studio likes it and decides to develop that idea into a pilot for a series.

The writer/producer writes the script for the pilot.

If the network/studio likes the pilot script, they give it the green light and begin the process of producing a pilot.

In December and January, a casting director (also with a great track record for working on pilots and series) is hired and creates a breakdown of the script for Breakdown Services. The breakdown will provide the following information: names of those producing, writing, and directing the pilot; the network and studio; the type of show (hour drama, multiple-camera sitcom, etc.); when the pilot will shoot and in what city; and most importantly, complete descriptions and requirements of all the roles to be cast. Should the pilot for an hour drama go to series, it may require casting of as many as ten series regulars (roles that appear in every episode).

Casting directors not only have to find actors for all of the series regulars for a pilot, but they also have to fill the co-star and guest star roles. That could be up to twenty actors for a pilot. The casting director traditionally has up to ten weeks to cast all the roles (although in the last few years the time-frame has narrowed down to four weeks or less).

During pilot season, which is traditionally January through March (but is changing as I write this – in fact some cable pilots are casting in June now), there is a lot of casting going on. It is a crazy, hectic time in which actors in high demand can be going out for two or three pilot auditions in a single day.

The order of auditions for any given pilot is as follows:

Pre-read with the casting director.

Callbacks for the producer/creator of the show.

A second callback for the producer, at which the producer will make very sure they like this actor.

If the actor makes it past this second callback, then the network/studio will start a test deal option. The test deal option starts negotiations between the agent representing the actor and the business affairs department of the network. The two parties will negotiate everything from billing to compensation for the pilot and for the series, and, if the pilot should go to series, dressing rooms, relocation fees, etc. This negotiation will lead to a contract that usually covers five to seven years. You will be working closely with your agent at this point as he/she negotiates with business affairs on your behalf.

The actor will sign this contract before going in to test at the studio. This test will be in front of the executives at the show's studio. Some examples of studios are Twentieth-Century Fox, Warner Brothers, and Paramount. The executives that will most likely be present are the President, the VP of Development, the VP of Casting, the Manager of Casting, and the Manager of Development who has been assigned to this particular show at that studio. It's a nerve-wracking audition and I've seen brilliant actors crumble under the pressure. The actor only gets this one chance. Those who do not do a great audition will not be hired. If it is for a comedy role and the actor doesn't get a laugh, they won't get hired.

If the actor does a great audition and if the executives fall in love with this actor, then the actor will proceed to the final audition in this grueling process – the network test. At the network test, the actor will audition for the President of, say, NBC. All the executives who were in the test at the studio will be at the network test, along with the VP of Development at NBC, the VP of Casting at NBC, the Manager of Casting at NBC, and so on.

Most of the time, there are three or four different actors vying for any one role at the studio. Usually, that gets narrowed down to two at the network. Some actors get cut at this point, and it is heartbreaking. However, if you're one of those cut, you will survive. Many, many fine actors through the years and years of pilot seasons were cut at this point. It does not mean they never worked again! They moved on and thrived.

For those actors who don't get cut, it is at the network test that one actor is hired for that role in that pilot. The executives of the studio and network see the auditions back to back and choose who they like the best. Sometimes they do not choose anyone and the casting director has to start back at square one for that role. That is a frustrating situation for everyone involved, but it does happen a lot. This is when we have to go back to the drawing board and want to pull our hair out.

If an actor is chosen at this test, he/she is hired to shoot the pilot as a series regular. The minimum they can make is $30,000 for fourteen days of work. $30,000 dollars for actors with no quotes, meaning, they have no fee quotes from another pilot. This is their first pilot. Most child actors who have never done a pilot will be paid this amount. The fees go up from there.

As recently as this current pilot season (2012), actors who don't live in either Los Angeles or New York, are going on tape and booking series regular jobs directly from these tapes. Emily Swallow, a very gifted actress who was doing a play, Cat on a Hot Tin Roof, at the Guthrie Theatre in Minneapolis, spent most of the days she was not performing the play putting herself on tape for many roles on new TV series. She booked one - "Chelsea General" (now titled "Monday Mornings") - produced by David E. Kelley for TNT, by using just a video camera the size of an iPhone. (It should be noted here that a casting director requested through her agent that she audition remotely.) Emily booked the pilot and the pilot got "picked up" for series. I'm very happy for her as she is a superb well-rounded actress.

Every actor wants to book a pilot. At the very least, they can make enough money to keep them going until their next union job. If the pilot goes to series and the actor's option is picked up (meaning that they're hired in that same role for the series), the actor is in position to make substantial money. They can make anywhere from $15,000 per episode (half their pilot fee) upwards. Most series that last a whole season make twenty-two episodes. Your agent will get ten percent of that money, and if you have a manager as well, he or she will get fifteen to twenty percent of that money, depending on what you have agreed beforehand.

Shows on cable, such as Disney, Nickelodeon, ABC Family, etc. do not pay as well as the networks – NBC, ABC, CBS, The CW, and Fox. But it's still a decent living.

Once a pilot is cast and shot the finished product is delivered to the network/studio, along with all the other pilots made during that pilot season. Some networks make ten to twenty pilots. All the pilots are assessed and it is at this time that the networks decide which of the pilots will go to series. It is also at this time that the actors who appeared in pilots find out whether they will have the good fortune to work on a series. The final announcements are unveiled at the up fronts which take place in New York City in mid-May. This is a huge event when all the advertisers and media buyers come to see what the new fall season will look like. Series production on the pilots that are picked up usually begins in July and August.

Most of the pilots that get made are never seen by the general public.

Here is a partial list of those pilots I worked on that never went forward:

"D.O.T.S." (Department of Transportation Services) - NBC - a show about meter maids, basically. I thought it was hilarious, but it was really more of a FOX show than for NBC. We did have to fire two of the actors after the first day of rehearsal. Never a good time.

"Sick in the Head" - FOX - created by Judd Apatow back in 1998 - starred David Krumholtz and Kevin Corrigan. Amy Poehler, before she did SNL, was a guest star on the pilot. Probably the funniest pilot ever made.

"All About Us" - CBS - Three couples all at various stages of a relationship. Yeah, it was pretty generic. It was tough finding the male leads, as is most often the case. They have to be naturally funny, attractive, and likable.

"Say Uncle" - CBS - Starred Ken Olin as a gay uncle who becomes the guardian to his sister's children after she's tragically killed in a car accident. Teri Hatcher was so great (she did this show before she got "Desperate Housewives" that really rejuvenated her career). Michael Angarano and Daveigh Chase were the kids and they were both brilliant.

"Misconceptions" - The WB - Jane Leeves plays a single mother who thirteen years prior had gone to a sperm back in order to conceive her child. Now that anonymous donor comes into her life. Taylor Momsen played the daughter. She had straight brown hair parted down the middle and wore no make-up. Times have changed for her.

I could go on, but frankly, I don't remember the names of half of them and it just makes me depressed thinking about all the hours I spent working on shows that never saw the light of day. Pilots that don't get picked up are as heartbreaking for the casting director as it is for the actors.

We give up so much of our personal lives during the casting process, it's ridiculous how we keep doing them.

Pilot season is a big deal and some actors organize their lives around it, hoping for that big break. For families and actors, going out to Los Angeles only for pilot season is tricky, however. Let's say you have a young female actress who can play between the ages of twelve and fifteen. You go out for pilot season on a particular year and it turns out for that pilot season that the shows do not happen to have roles in her age range. You do not know if this will be the case until you're already out there and the breakdowns start coming out. Does this mean you have wasted all that time and money being out in Los Angeles for pilot season? Not necessarily. You can make the most of your time out there by enrolling your daughter in good acting classes, doing casting director workshops, and auditioning for roles on TV shows that are already on the air or a studio film that will get distribution.

Pilot season is great, but booking a pilot your first season out is like winning the Lottery. It's fantastic when it happens but it's not something you can count on. What's more important for a working actor is the entire TV season – July through March – when all the shows are in production.

Recently, it's come to my attention that the term "pilot" can sometimes be bandied about by folks trying to appear more important than they are or to elevate the status of a project that is nothing more than a homemade video.

A "pilot" as it relates to network TV's annual "pilot season" is the first episode of a TV show that might or might not become a series. If it's picked up by the network, it becomes a series and the pilot is broadcast. If the series is not picked up, than the pilot goes into the black hole of past pilots, usually never to see the light of day.

If a producer says they have a "pilot," that should mean that it's under the umbrella of a network and studio (20th Century Fox for NBC, for instance) and that the network is paying the tab.

What infuriates me is when someone says they are making a pilot but there is no network or studio attached already. In fact, what often happens in smaller market is that a producer will self-finance a short video in the hopes of selling the idea to a network or cable channel. They will call it a "pilot," but it really isn't. One is more likely to win the lottery than to sell a spec pilot to a network.

For the most part, the networks are in development with writer-producers who already have a track record of writing for shows that have been on the air. There is so much money involved in financing a TV show these days that a network is unlikely to take a chance on an unknown.

Recently, I received a frantic email from a good friend of mine, Shelly Gaza, who teaches acting at The University of Northern Colorado in Greeley. A talented student of hers, Abby, had been contacted by a former colleague, Michael, who was helping to cast a "pilot" through Metal Flowers Media. He told Abby that she would be right for it and asked if she wanted to submit for it, which of course she did straight away. What a chance of a lifetime! She was sent some sides in October of 2011 and subsequently put on tape by Michael. She was also sent a photo of the other actress up for the same role.

At this point, Abby hadn't see a breakdown or a full script, nor did she do any online research to find out if this was all legitimate. Why would she? Michael was not a stranger to her but someone she knew, who was aware of how talented she was. All he had to do was say the magical word "pilot" and Abby, a usually very smart person, became a dupe.

In December, Abby was told by Michael that she had booked a pilot for NBC (!) and was "on avail" for May 15th - 21st. She was also told her salary would be $200,000+ for the first season. Abby was very excited about this news, to say the least.

Michael sent her a Non-Disclosure Agreement to sign as she did not have an agent.

This is when Shelly, her professor, thought this whole thing sounded dubious and too-good-to-be-true. She contacted me to get my perspective. Upon hearing the whole story, I connected with Michael via email and realized quite quickly that this was all some sort of scheme to either meet women and/or seem a power player in the Hollywood scene. As it turns out, Michael was duped as well, by someone he trusted but shouldn't have.

Of course, Abby is mortified, frustrated, and angered by this turn-of-events. Sadly, I'm sure she's not the only actress to have ever been manipulated in this way. I pray to God she will be the last, at least for those who read this book.

She went on to contact Metal Flowers Media herself and found out that Michael had left the company back in December and that they didn't know anything about an NBC pilot or a contract for $200,000+.

What are the lessons to be learned from this? First off, don't trust anyone, even a colleague, who says they are casting a pilot. This is pretty pie-in-the-sky and you must make sure it's real before embarking on it. In hindsight, Abby should have googled Metal Flowers Media as soon as she got off the phone with Michael the first time.

If you do find yourself auditioning for a casting director of a pilot, do your research first. Find the casting director's credits on IMDB. Call their office to confirm. Go to the websites www.deadlinehollywood.com or www.thefutoncritic.com to confirm that indeed a pilot is being produced by a network with the title of the project you are going on tape for.

Ask for the breakdown of the project published by Breakdown Services. Every single pilot under the umbrella of a network or cable channel, without exception, will have a breakdown stating all the details - as has been already discussed in an earlier chapter.

Know the timeline of the majority of network pilots. The fact that the presumed pilot was shooting May 15th - 21st was a dead giveaway right there. That's the week of the up fronts, when the pilots that have been picked up for series are announced to the press and media outlets. No pilot will ever be shooting during that time.

Finally, you'll never be put "on avail" unless you've tested at the studio and signed a contract in which everything is spelled out in detail.

The quintessential discussion on pilot season from the actor's perspective is "The Actors' Pilot Season Plight," an audiocast to be found on the KCRW website - www.kcrw.com. - as part of a series entitled *The Business.*

The Business is the show about the business of show business. It goes beyond the glitz and glamour to the who, what, why and how of making movies and TV. The Business is hosted by respected entertainment industry journalist Kim Masters of the Hollywood Reporter and produced by Darby Maloney at KCRW. Each week The Business features an analysis of top Hollywood news with John Horn of the Los Angeles Times, in-depth interviews and the occasional feature story.

Special Permission to Include Audiocast of this Episode in the digital versions of this book, graciously provided by KCRW 89.9

chapter ten

My Final Words

I have spent eighteen years – and still counting – in The Room. There are times when it is heartbreaking and there are times when magic happens. Despite the time I've spent feeling bored out of my mind, there have been more times in which I got goose bumps and was emotionally moved. I laughed, I cried, I helped thousands of actors pursue their passion and hundreds of directors and writers see their projects come to life.

As with so many aspects of life, I sometimes ask what is this all for, really? Are the costs, compromises, and countless hours spent in The Room all finally worth it? As I said previously, there is a large cost that your family ends up paying for you to pursue your passion, and my daughter, Kate, paid a high price.

As it is with any endeavor, "it was the best of times and it was the worst of times." I have a great life and am grateful for all that has happened to me, the good and the not-so-good.

Fulfilling your wildest dreams will not change the facts of your childhood. It never brought my dad back to life, and it won't make your family less dysfunctional.

If you become desperate and needy, thinking that you'll never book jobs and envious of actors who do, it's time to get out of the business. The casting directors will smell your self-defeat a mile away and will not hire you.

Please have sympathy for the casting directors. We get as nervous as you do in The Room. We are under more pressure and stress than you can imagine. Remember to always make it about the other person and make The Room about us and not you.

Why is it that some actors become very successful and others do not? What do you do if you have insurmountable obstacles to overcome? What if you're very talented but crippled with insecurity? What exactly do you do with the information if you're told you're too tall or that you're too old to get an agent? What if someone thinks your calves are too big? What if you're an Asian actress and all the roles available to you are either prostitutes or nerds?

The reality is that any and all actors have "limitations." Very few actors and actresses are the embodiment of the physical "ideal" human being. Regardless of skin color, shape of the eye, weight, or sexual orientation, and in spite of the worlds prejudices and biases, it's your job to change our minds. In order to get work, you will have to shake up preconceived notions of how certain characters are to be portrayed.

The truth is that all of us have our individual stories and deep down, we're interested in each other. We are all fascinated by other people and casting directors make a living at looking into the souls of all kinds of people from all walks of life. If you don't let us in because of insecurities, however, we won't see you, and that's a damn shame.

My wish for the third edition of this book is that I'll be writing about the over abundance of diverse actors on TV. I hope that one day soon the faces I see on the small and big screens will reflect in equal amounts the mix of people I see in American sports, the music industry, and just plain walking around in my world in Santa Monica.

In parting, let me emphatically stress yet again that the following are precepts you must live by if you want to be in the game:

You must master The Room. Being in The Room is like being in the finals at Wimbledon. You can't blow a single point. You have to be in your zone and hit every single ball with all that you have in you.

You must know who you are, the dark side as well as the light, and be comfortable with all aspects of your personality. You can't be someone you're not, even if you have buckets of money to spend on plastic surgery. You have to be genuine and believable. Being a great actor is not about pretense. Ironic, isn't it? So many people go into acting because they love to pretend they're someone else. In reality, those who succeed are able to reveal who they already are – the good, the bad, and the ugly.

There was a working actor I liked a lot. I brought him in The Room for a pilot. He was of indeterminate sexual orientation, slight of build, had very crooked yellow teeth, and was not attractive in any traditional sense of the word. His forte was comedy, however, and he made The Room laugh. The producers and I simply sat back and enjoyed his presence, his humor, and his lack of pretense. It did not matter that he was not traditionally attractive; he was beautiful to us in that moment. As one of the producers pointed out to me, "being funny trumps bad teeth any day."

If you cannot look in the mirror without cringing, or can't bear being by yourself for even a whole day, don't go into acting. Acting is facing who you are all of the time.

You must possess a life force.   If you don't have passion, desire, and charisma, why should we spend time in The Room with you? Being in the room with an actor who has no charisma is demoralizing to us. We can't be emotionally moved by an actor who is not passionate.

With charisma, you eventually will succeed, even if your calves are big or you're too old to get an agent. Charisma trumps height, old age, and bad teeth. Look at Alison Janney, Kathy Joosten (RIP), and John C. Reilly.

If you're not getting the attention of agents or casting directors, then create your own work.   There are so many ways to be seen these days, what with the low cost of creating your own webseries or short film, as well as open mic nights all around the city where you can read your own poetry, do stand-up, or sing.   Don't sit around lamenting the dearth of opportunities otherwise you will not be a pleasant person to be around if and when you do get an audition.

You are all the casting director has. We don't write the scripts, we don't design the sets, all we do is find actors. You are the sole reflection of all our hard work and passion. So, when you go in The Room, remember that and make us all look brilliant. We love you, you know.

Summary of Top Ten Secrets of Charisma

1. Reveal Your NATURAL SEXINESS And You'll Own The Room. There is nothing like looking into your lover's face and seeing his or her eyes look at you in "that way." They are open, relaxed, reflecting a positive energy and desire. We can't help but be drawn into that. If you can convey your natural sexiness without being gross about it, you will own us. Your natural sexiness is the true you in a relaxed state. Try flirting with your audience. Look at them with love not fear.

2. Create CHEMISTRY In The Room by Making It About The Other Person. You don't want to be a selfish lover, then don't be a selfish leader/actor. Whatever you have to say is about the other person, whether it is the other character in the scene or your audience. That is why you're there in the first place – what is your relationship to them? How do you feel about them? What do you want from them? It's the chemistry that happens between people that creates magic.

3. Express VULNERABILITY To Exude Magnetism. The more we can see your vulnerability, your humanness, your reflection of the human condition, the more we are drawn in to you. Good actors are brave folks. They go emotionally where we are afraid to go. That's why we want to watch them so much. Good leaders have the same quality. Is your Public Persona different from your Private Persona? Try showing more sadness, more fear, more genuine humor in your Public Side.

4. Control the ADRENALINE RUSH To Increase Your Personal Power. It's your job to make your audience comfortable so they can enjoy and listen to what you have to say. If you're nervous, we'll feel sorry for you, we will feel compassion but we won't be moved to take action. Some ways to combat nerves: Yoga, Meditation, Hypnotherapy (www.stephanie-jones.com)

5. **ALL WE WANT IS YOU**. It doesn't matter how cute you are or who you know, if your audience can't connect to you as a person, they won't be interested. If you're a different person in your presentation than you are when you initially walked in The Room, the YOU who walked in The Room will be the one we want to connect with. Are you emotionally blocked, not being genuine?

6. **Be a Good LISTENER and Connect With Your Audience Powerfully.** First rule of Dating and Relationships. It's the communication between people that moves us. Are you talking at us or simply talking to us? Stop thinking about how you're doing and just be present.

7. **Show HUMILITY To Create Lasting Relationships.** Be Confident, not arrogant. There is a huge difference. Confidence is when you're sure of yourself, when you feel comfortable in your own skin. Arrogance is when you don't feel sure of yourself, but you're acting as if you do. As in dating, this is one of the biggest turn-offs there is. And actors who are slick and "act" make us want to run out of The Room.

8. **DON'T THINK SO MUCH In Order To Avoid Self-Consciousness**. If you start analyzing your work/speech as you're doing it, you will kill the spontaneity. Your audience can tell when you're not present in the moment and preoccupied. Good preparation and feeling good about what you're doing are the keys to conquering your self-consciousness. Also, just being comfortable in your own skin. Maybe a good Improvisation class would be good for you. It works with actors who are "too tight."

9. **DON'T TRY HARD to Be A Leader, JUST BE.** Try too hard to make us like you and you'll turn us away. Try too hard to be good, and you'll just get tired. Great athletes make it look easy. There has to be an "ease" in everything you do, otherwise you will make your audience uncomfortable. If you've ever seen wannabe comic actors trying to BE FUNNY in order to get on a sitcom, you'll know what I mean. There's a desperation there that is not pretty.

10. **Be HEALTHY EMOTIONALLY and PHYSICALLY And Be A Hero.** In order to be around for the long haul, you must be healthy in every way. The Ideal Actor or Leader is the Ideal Person. Your audience looks up to you. They admire you. You are the representative of humanity. You have a great responsibility. Eat right, exercise, and go to therapy! Don't make the excuse you don't have time. You won't have time if you don't do these things

Made in the USA
Lexington, KY
29 September 2013